Cognitive-Behavioral Stress Management

Cognitive-Behavioral Stress Management

Workbook

Michael H. Antoni • Gail Ironson • Neil Schneiderman

OXFORD

UNIVERSITY PRESS

2007

OXFORD
UNIVERSITY PRESS

Oxford University Press, Inc., publishes works that further
Oxford University's objective of excellence
in research, scholarship, and education.

Oxford   New York
Auckland   Cape Town   Dar es Salaam   Hong Kong   Karachi
Kuala Lumpur   Madrid   Melbourne   Mexico City   Nairobi
New Delhi   Shanghai   Taipei   Toronto

With offices in
Argentina   Austria   Brazil   Chile   Czech Republic   France   Greece
Guatemala   Hungary   Italy   Japan   Poland   Portugal   Singapore
South Korea   Switzerland   Thailand   Turkey   Ukraine   Vietnam

Published by Oxford University Press, Inc.
198 Madison Avenue, New York, New York 10016

www.oup.com

Oxford is a registered trademark of Oxford University Press

ISBN 978-0-19-532790-8

Printed in the United States of America
on acid-free paper

About Treatments*ThatWork*™

One of the most difficult problems confronting patients with various disorders and diseases is finding the best help available. Everyone is aware of friends or family who have sought treatment from a seemingly reputable practitioner, only to find out later from another doctor that the original diagnosis was wrong or the treatments recommended were inappropriate or perhaps even harmful. Most patients, or family members, address this problem by reading everything they can about their symptoms, seeking out information on the Internet, or aggressively "asking around" to tap knowledge from friends and acquaintances. Governments and healthcare policymakers are also aware that people in need don't always get the best treatments—something they refer to as "variability in healthcare practices."

Now healthcare systems around the world are attempting to correct this variability by introducing "evidence-based practice." This simply means that it is in everyone's interest that patients get the most up-to-date and effective care for a particular problem. Healthcare policymakers have also recognized that it is very useful to give consumers of healthcare as much information as possible, so that they can make intelligent decisions in a collaborative effort to improve health and mental health. This series, Treatments *ThatWork*™, is designed to accomplish just that. Only the latest and most effective interventions for particular problems are described, in user-friendly language. To be included in this series, each treatment program must pass the highest standards of evidence available, as determined by a scientific advisory board. Thus, when individuals suffering from these problems or their family members seek out an expert clinician who is familiar with these interventions and decides that they are appropriate, they will have confidence that they are receiving the best care available. Of course, only your healthcare professional can decide on the right mix of treatments for you.

This group program is designed to help individuals living with HIV deal with stress and improve quality of life. It provides proven methods to manage stress and induce relaxation. In this program, you will learn skills to increase your awareness of stress and your ability to effectively cope with it. You will also learn a wide array of relaxation methods, so you can choose the techniques that work best for you. Using relaxation and stress management techniques in your daily life can reduce your stress levels, which can help maintain healthy immune functioning. Your participation in this program can have important benefits for your life and your health. This program is most effective when carried out in collaboration with a trained facilitator.

David H. Barlow, Editor-in-Chief
Treatments *That Work*™
Boston, Massachusetts

Contents

Chapter 1

Overview of the Program

Goals

- To learn about what this program involves
- To understand the structure of the sessions

General Program Information

This program focuses on stress management techniques and relaxation skills. You will be learning to deal with stress in a healthy and effective manner. You probably experience stressful work, home, or social situations in your daily life; most people do at least every so often. Even if you do not consider your life to be very stressful, you can still benefit from this program. For example, you can apply the skills taught in this program to making decisions or communicating more effectively in all kinds of situations, not just stressful ones. At those times when you do experience stress, the techniques you will learn will help you to cope.

Attendance

It is important that you attend every session in this program. Each session will build on the stress management and relaxation skills taught in the previous session. If you are unable to attend a session, speak to one of the group leaders about what you can do to keep up with the group.

Confidentiality

Keeping information about other group members confidential is a requirement of belonging to this group. Confidentiality is necessary so that participants can speak naturally in the group, without worrying that others will find out about what they said. You can feel free to talk about your own experiences or feelings with people outside of the group, but please don't talk about other members' experiences even without using their names. You may have friends or acquaintances in common, even if you are not aware of it. Sometimes people can guess from the context whom you are talking about, and there goes the group's confidentiality. When sharing what you are learning in group with family and friends, be careful to speak only of your own experiences and not the experiences of others in the group.

Session Structure and Use of the Workbook

Each session will consist of two parts. One part will cover stress management techniques and the other part will teach relaxation exercises. The material in this workbook corresponds to what you will be learning in group. It includes exercises that you will be completing during group meetings, as well as homework forms. After each session, you will want to review the corresponding chapter in the workbook and complete the homework.

Stress Management Techniques

This part of the session will usually begin with group discussion of stressful situations, issues related to sexual orientation, and issues related to AIDS. Some of the topics you will be discussing may be uncomfortable or anxiety-producing; you may prefer not to talk or hear about them at all. In that case, it is all right to limit your participation; however, it is important for you to be present for every discussion. Let the group leaders know if you are feeling anxious or uncomfortable with a topic. They will work with you to learn how to handle the anxiety so you can take in the information the group is providing. Remember that a lot of your learning in this program will come from listening and sharing with other group members.

Many of the things you will be learning in the coming weeks involve a set of psychological techniques collectively referred to as Cognitive-

Behavioral Stress Management (CBSM). Some of these procedures are designed to increase your awareness of the link between the ways in which you think about stressful events and how you feel. You will learn ways to change your thinking in order to modify your emotional responses. The "Behavioral" in CBSM refers to what you actually do about stressors—your coping strategies. You will learn to become more aware of some inefficient and indirect strategies (e.g., substance use, overeating, drinking) that you may have developed for dealing with painful or stressful challenges. You will start to replace these with more healthy, efficient, and direct strategies. In addition, anger management techniques will help you to learn healthier ways to handle and express angry feelings. Assertiveness training will help you to develop better strategies for confronting others, protecting your personal rights, and expressing your needs. Finally, other techniques will help you to become more aware of the social resources that are available to you. You will learn ways to increase the size and usefulness of your existing social support network. Together, these techniques address the four components of stress management.

Four Components of Stress Management

1. Awareness: *How we react to stress*

2. Appraisals: *What we think about stress*

3. Coping: *What we do about stress*

4. Resources: *What helps us manage stress*

During the sessions, you will be engaging in exercises to help you to learn the different techniques. You will also be asked to complete homework assignments practicing these techniques. These will be very practical, like paying attention to your stress levels and what you say to yourself and how you feel when you're stressed. Most people find these exercises both interesting and useful. The weekly homework assignments are just as important as the group meetings: it is necessary for you to complete them in order to get the most benefit from the program.

The other component of each session teaches relaxation exercises. The first relaxation technique, progressive muscle relaxation (PMR), will help you to learn to relax your muscles whenever you want to. This will help you to release tension from the body and may help you to feel better in general. In later sessions, you will learn deep breathing techniques and relaxation self-suggestions called autogenic training, as well as some imagery and meditation techniques. After you learn all the techniques, you can use whatever you like best in the future.

In order for this program to be most effective, you will need to practice relaxation at home on a regular basis. Once you learn a relaxation technique, you will be asked to practice every day during the following weeks. You will need to find time in your schedule to do this every day to get the most benefit from the technique.

Chapter 2

Session 1: Stressors and Stress Responses /
Progressive Muscle Relaxation
for 16 Muscle Groups

Overview

At the beginning of the first session, you will learn about the program and get to know the other group members. The next part of the session introduces the first component of stress management, which involves becoming aware of your stressors and your physical stress responses. In the last part of the session, you will practice the first relaxation exercise, Progressive Muscle Relaxation for 16 Muscle Groups.

Getting Acquainted Exercise

During the first part of the session, your group leaders will ask you to interview another group member. You will then make a short presentation to the group about what you have learned about your partner.

You may use the following questions in the interview. Write down your partner's answers in the space provided.

Partner's Name: _____

■ What are your hobbies? _____

_____

■ What do you like to do on the weekend? _____

_____

■ How would your family and friends describe you? _____

_____

After the interview, list three adjectives that describe your partner (e.g., smart, funny, creative) and include these in your presentation to the group.

My partner is:

1. _____

2. _____

3. _____

STRESS MANAGEMENT: *Stressors and Stress Responses*

Goals

- To generate a list of stressors in your life

- To understand the definition of stress

- To become aware of the physical effects of stress

- To learn about the possible health consequences of stress

Generating a List of Stressors

Think about what makes you feel stressed and when. The chart on page 7 will help you get in touch with some of the ways you respond to common situations. Start out with some everyday examples—not big things, just the small hassles that seem to recur on a regular basis. Recall the events of the past week or two and make a list of the stressful events that happened in the left-hand column. In the right-hand column write the ways in which you experienced the events as stressful.

What Is Stress?

Stress has been defined several ways:

- An external event

- A discomfort or tension

Event	My Experiences
Bad drivers on the road	I was angry and frustrated. My body felt tense.

- One's reaction to an event or state

- The way in which all of these things interact

Behavioral scientists call the event that triggers a stressful reaction a stressor. Stress is thought of as what the individual experiences in response to this stressor. Not everyone finds the same situations stressful or experiences stress in the same way. For example, for some people going to the doctor triggers a stressful reaction, while for others it may not cause any problems. Some people experience anger, depression, or anxiety when they are stressed. Others have physical symptoms such as headaches, tightness in the chest, upset stomach, or muscle tension.

Physical Effects of Stress

When you encounter a stressful situation, a variety of physiological responses take place. To start off, your senses or sensory organs—eyes, ears, and so on—send information to your brain. There, the highest part of your brain, the cortex, interprets the information; this is where what you are thinking and feeling about the situation takes place. If the information is interpreted as stressful, then lower parts of the brain set off a complex physiological response that involves glands and organs of the whole body.

Fight-or-Flight Response

The first set of responses is caused by messages being sent to body organs via the nervous system. This is often called the "fight-or-flight" response, because it prepares your body to either attack or run. This response was adaptive for our ancestors when they faced a hungry lion. It is still useful for us today when we need to take quick physical action in response to a stressor—for example, getting out of the way of a moving car.

The following are some physical changes that are part of the "fight-or-flight" response:

- Pupils dilate
- Respiration increases
- Heart rate increases
- Blood pressure increases
- Blood flows to muscles away from organs
- Sweat glands are stimulated
- Sugar and fatty acids are released into blood
- Adrenal gland releases adrenaline

Because the information involved in stress processing travels over nerves, these physical effects occur quickly—in almost the same instant that you interpret something as stressful. The body is ready to take action immediately: increased heart rate and respiration allow more oxygen to be available to cells, sugar and fatty acids provide energy to the cells, and so on.

My Physical Effects of Stress

Review the list of physical changes associated with the "fight-or-flight" response. How many of these stress signs have you been aware of? Which ones are relatively common occurrences for you? How often? Complete the chart on page 9.

Example: My heart races	# times/month: 8
Sign #1:	# times/month:
Sign #2:	# times/month:

Other Bodily Changes

Another set of responses that takes place involves glands and hormones. The pituitary gland under the brain releases a hormone into the bloodstream. This hormone travels to the adrenal gland, which is located above the kidney, and tells it to release a group of hormones called corticosteroids. The corticosteroids are important in the stress response because they help relieve damage. For example, they can reduce fever, inflammation, or tissue damage. These hormones also help in sugar production so energy will be available to the cells.

Another group of chemicals that is released under stressful conditions are called endogenous opiates because they act like opiate drugs (e.g., morphine). These chemicals are helpful in reducing pain associated with injury and exertion. These chemicals act as a pain reliever so that the person can continue to defend himself if he is injured during a fight. Or, if the person is running away from danger, he won't need to stop because he won't feel the pain. The endogenous opiates help us not only physically but also mentally. They can give you a sense of well-being—for example, a "runner's high."

Possible Health Consequences of Stress

When a stressor activates the fight-or-flight response, your heart rate increases, your adrenaline starts to flow, sugar and fatty acids are released, and so forth. These events all prepare the body to take some sort of physical action against the stressor. But in our society physical action isn't usually the best way to deal with the stresses we encounter. For example, if your boss is asking you to do extra work, it isn't to your advantage to hit him or to run away. Your body still responds, however, as if these were possible options. The physiological changes that then take place can have lasting effects on the body.

We know the most about how these changes affect the cardiovascular system. For example, the fatty acids that are released into the blood wind up not being used, because you are not taking physical action. So these fats hang around in your bloodstream and may contribute to the development of atherosclerosis (hardening of the arteries). Also, the unused adrenaline and noradrenaline may cause damage to the blood vessel walls, which can make these walls vulnerable to hardening of the arteries and clotting as well.

In people who are vulnerable to hypertension (high blood pressure), the increase in blood pressure during stress may persist over the years, leading to hypertension, which in turn can lead to strokes. Also, in people whose heart muscles are already weakened (say from hardened arteries), the increase in heart rate during the stress response can lead to heart attacks.

Physical changes during stress also appear to affect the gastrointestinal tract. You are probably aware that sometimes people under a lot of stress develop ulcers or stomach acid conditions—for example, the stereotypical executive who has to take Maalox.

Immune Functioning Responses

Stress seems to negatively affect immune functioning. For example, studies have shown that students are more susceptible to viruses around exam time and people are more likely to catch colds when they've been under stress. This is because stress weakens the cells and antibodies that protect you against viruses. Other immune cells—natural killer cells, which are important in fighting tumor cells and viruses—seem to decrease their activity when the body is under stress. Elevations in the body's stress hormones such as corticosteroids and adrenaline have been associated with decreases in immune function. This stress-related immunosuppression may compound the preexisting immunosuppression found in HIV-infected individuals. In addition, it has been found that the ability of HIV-1 to infect normal human lymphocytes (e.g., T cells) is increased when corticosteroids are added.

The following model (figure 2.1) demonstrates the relationship between stress, immune functioning, and HIV disease progression. When we encounter stressors we first "process" them in the brain through cognitive appraisals, planned coping strategies, and affective (emotional) changes. The nervous system then responds by stimulating production of adrenal stress hormones. These stress hormones help prepare our bodies to deal with challenges through "fight or flight"; however, they also tend to decrease the immune system's ability to combat viral infections and cancerous cells. In the case of HIV infection, stressors and the ways they are processed may contribute to accelerated disease progression through their effects on immune functioning.

The hormonal and immunological changes that occur in response to stress are typically accompanied by symptoms of distress: anxiety,

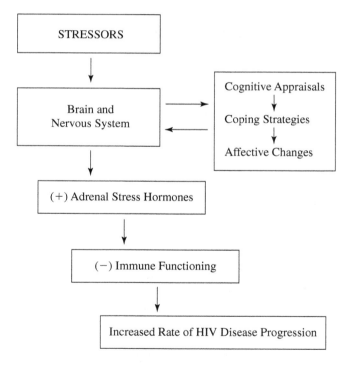

Figure 2.1

Stressors and HIV disease progression

depression, loneliness, and social isolation. Studies examining the effects of loneliness, marriage problems, lack of social support, bereavement, and the stress of HIV antibody testing itself have found significant relationships between these stressors and changes in hormone levels, immune function, and psychological and emotional well-being. Stress management techniques and relaxation exercises, however, may help reduce the impact of these stressors by decreasing one's stress level. In the case of HIV infection the benefits of stress management may have direct implications for staying well.

This CBSM program is intended to increase your sense of control, self-efficacy, self-esteem, adaptive coping, and social support. These

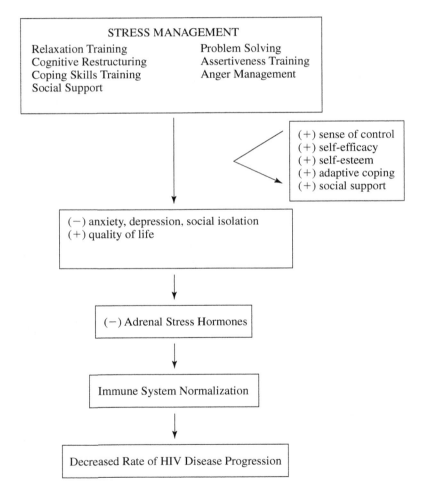

Figure 2.2

Stress management and HIV disease progression

changes are thought to decrease negative mood states and social isolation and increase quality of life. As a result, stress hormone levels may decrease and the immune system may be able to maintain normal functioning. The model in figure 2.2 demonstrates how stress management may contribute to a decreased rate of HIV disease progression.

RELAXATION TRAINING: *Progressive Muscle Relaxation for 16 Muscle Groups*

Goals

- To learn about progressive muscle relaxation (PMR)
- To practice PMR for 16 muscle groups daily
- To monitor your stress levels

Introduction to Progressive Muscle Relaxation (PMR)

Often, people develop physical tension when they encounter stressful and even not-so-stressful events. You may have noticed tightness in your muscles or excess tension in your body. To reduce this tension, you will learn a process called progressive muscle relaxation training or PMR. PMR training consists of learning how to tense and release various muscle groups throughout the body to decrease physical tension. By practicing this method every day you will train your muscles to relax so less physical tension will develop.

Progressive muscle relaxation was first developed in the 1930s as people explored how tensing of muscles can be related to other physiological changes in the body. At the same time that muscles tense, hormones and other chemicals are released in the body. Physical changes follow, such as an increased heart rate and increased blood flow to the arms and legs. These responses can be useful if the stress we are dealing with is one that requires a physical response, such as jumping out of the way of a car or fighting off an attacker. As you've learned, this set of physical responses is often referred to as the "fight-or-flight" response. When these reactions are very frequent or occur over longer periods, they can have negative effects on the body. One way to prevent this is to learn how to turn off the "fight-or-flight" response through PMR.

Not only can PMR help to maintain your physical health, but many people find that if they reduce tension, they can work more effectively, enjoy life more, and appreciate their social life to a greater extent.

Instructions for Progressive Muscle Relaxation

After you have learned PMR in session, use the following instructions to practice PMR at home. Practice the PMR exercise every day. Regular practice is the key to making relaxation work for you. If you are having trouble fitting relaxation into your schedule, use the Activity Log on page 16 to find time available when you could practice.

Begin by choosing a quiet location where you will not be disturbed. Make yourself comfortable and loosen any tight clothing.

You should tense each muscle group for 10 seconds. Then release the tension and relax the muscle group for about 20 seconds, saying the word "relax" silently to yourself with each exhale of the breath. Focus on the difference between the sensations of tension and relaxation.

After tensing and releasing the 16 muscle groups, count from one to five to deepen relaxation. Breathe slowly for two minutes, repeating the word "relax" with every exhalation. Then count from five to one to return to a state of alertness.

The following describes how to create tension in each muscle group:

1, 2. Lower arms: make fists and pull up the wrists

3, 4. Upper arms: pull your arms back and in toward your sides

5, 6. Lower legs: flex your feet and pull your toes toward your upper body

7, 8. Upper legs: pull your knees together and lift your legs off the floor

9. Stomach: pull your stomach in toward your spine very tightly

10. Chest: take a deep breath and hold it

11. Shoulders: imagine your shoulders are on strings and are pulled up toward your ears

12. Neck: press your neck back and pull your chin down toward your chest

13. Mouth, jaw, throat: clench your teeth and force the corners of your mouth back into a forced smile

14. Eyes: squeeze your eyes tightly shut for a few seconds

15. Lower forehead: frown, pulling your eyebrows down and toward the center

16. Upper forehead: raise your eyebrows as high as you can

Remember, if you experience pain or discomfort when tensing a muscle group, release the tension immediately. Try tensing less the next time or only do the relaxing part of the exercise for that muscle group.

Before and after each relaxation practice, record your stress level on the Daily Self-Monitoring Sheet. You may photocopy this form from the book or download multiple copies from the Treatments *That-Work*™ Web site at www.oup.com/us/ttw. You will also use this form to record your stress levels throughout the day. Pick four specific times to monitor your stress levels every day. Each time, rate your stress level on a scale from one to seven. At the end of the day, rate your overall stress level for the day.

Homework

✎ Fill out the Activity Log on two separate days. Schedule relaxation as a regular part of your daily routine.

✎ Practice PMR for 16 Muscle Groups on a daily basis (twice a day if possible). Record stress levels before and after each practice on the Daily Self-Monitoring Sheet.

✎ Monitor your stress levels at specified times each day and record on the Daily Self-Monitoring Sheet.

Activity Log

Please record what you did on two separate days. You can either record the activities as you do them or record them at the end of the day.

Date _____   **Date** _____

Morning   **Activities**   **Activities**

_____   _____   _____

_____   _____   _____

_____   _____   _____

Afternoon

_____   _____   _____

_____   _____   _____

_____   _____   _____

_____   _____   _____

Evening

_____   _____   _____

_____   _____   _____

_____   _____   _____

_____   _____   _____

Source: Adapted from M. Davis, E. Eshelman, & M. McKay, *The Relaxation and Stress Reduction Workbook* (Oakland, CA: New Harbinger, 1988).

Daily Self-Monitoring Sheet

Use the following scale to indicate your stress level:

Not at all stressed   As stressed as you can be

Daily Stress Level

	Sunday	Monday	Tuesday	Wednesday	Thursday	Friday	Saturday
Time 1:	Rating:	Rating:	Rating:	Rating:	Rating:	Rating:	Rating:
Time 2:	Rating:	Rating:	Rating:	Rating:	Rating:	Rating:	Rating:
Time 3:	Rating:	Rating:	Rating:	Rating:	Rating:	Rating:	Rating:
Time 4:	Rating:	Rating:	Rating:	Rating:	Rating:	Rating:	Rating:
Day Overall	Rating:	Rating:	Rating:	Rating:	Rating:	Rating:	Rating:

Relaxation Practice

	Sunday	Monday	Tuesday	Wednesday	Thursday	Friday	Saturday
Exercise:	Before: After:	Before: After:	Before: After:	Before: After:	Before: After:	Before: After:	Before: After:
Exercise:	Before: After:	Before: After:	Before: After:	Before: After:	Before: After:	Before: After:	Before: After:
Exercise:	Before: After:	Before: After:	Before: After:	Before: After:	Before: After:	Before: After:	Before: After:
Exercise:	Before: After:	Before: After:	Before: After:	Before: After:	Before: After:	Before: After:	Before: After:
Exercise:	Before: After:	Before: After:	Before: After:	Before: After:	Before: After:	Before: After:	Before: After:

Chapter 3

Session 2: Stress and Awareness / Progressive Muscle Relaxation for Eight Muscle Groups

Overview

In this session you will learn about how stress can affect your thought patterns, your emotional state, your behavior, your physical sensations and tension levels, and the ways in which you relate to others. The importance of awareness for stress management will be discussed. During the session you will participate in exercises to help you to become more aware of your physical symptoms and their connection to your thoughts and feelings. You will also continue practicing progressive muscle relaxation, but now with only eight muscle groups instead of 16.

STRESS MANAGEMENT: *Stress and Awareness*

Goals

- To become aware of the effects of stress

- To understand the importance of awareness for stress management

- To increase awareness of physical responses to stressors

The Effects of Stress

Last session, we defined stress as an individual's response to an external event that is perceived as exceeding her capacity to handle. The stress response can affect the way we think, the way we feel, and the way we act. It can also have an impact on our bodies and our relationships with others. The effects of stress fall into five main categories:

- *Cognitive:* anxious thoughts, fearful anticipation, poor concentration, difficulty with memory

- *Emotional:* feelings of tension, worries, irritability, feelings of restlessness, inability to relax, depression

- *Behavioral:* avoidance of tasks, sleep problems, difficulty in completing work assignments, changes in drinking, eating, or smoking behaviors

- *Physical:* stiff muscles, teeth grinding, clenching fists, sweating, tension headaches, feeling faint, choking feeling, difficulty swallowing, stomachache, loss of interest in sex, tiredness, awareness of heart beating

- *Social:* avoiding others, isolating oneself, seeking out other people, venting, getting easily irritated with others

The checklist on page 21 will help you be more aware of your personal responses to stress. You can refer back to this list periodically to see how your responses change over time. It is important to become aware of these various effects of stress. They can be used as cues for when you need to find better coping strategies.

Stress and Awareness

Stress management helps us become more aware of situations that cause stress and provides effective techniques for coping with stress. Many times we have no control over the occurrence of stressful situations. However, we can get control over the ways that we deal with stress, which can either increase or decrease our stress symptoms. First, though, we must become aware of how stress symptoms are affected by our thoughts and emotions.

Awareness of Automatic Thoughts

Automatic thoughts are the first thoughts we experience in a situation; they occur so quickly they feel "automatic." They occur before we can "catch" ourselves and represent a habitual way of responding to stressful circumstances. Since these thoughts happen so fast, our emotional responses seem to come out of the blue.

Symptoms of Stress Checklist

Check the stress-related symptoms below that apply to you. Rate each for the degree of discomfort it causes you, using a 10-point scale: 1 = little distress; 10 = extreme distress. Disregard those you don't experience.

Hostility:	_____	Anger:	_____
Irritability:	_____	Resentment:	_____
Phobias:	_____	Fears:	_____
Obsessions:	_____	Muscular tension:	_____
Headaches:	_____	Neckaches:	_____
Backaches:	_____	Indigestion:	_____
Irritable bowel:	_____	Ulcers:	_____
Constipation:	_____	Chronic diarrhea:	_____
Muscle spasms:	_____	Nervous tics:	_____
Insomnia:	_____	Sleeping problems:	_____
Obesity:	_____	Physical weakness:	_____
Depression:	_____	Low self-esteem:	_____
Withdrawal:	_____	Drinking/Drug use:	_____
Other:_____		Other: _____	

Source: Adapted from M. Davis, E. Eshelman, & M. McKay, *The Relaxation and Stress Reduction Workbook* (Oakland, CA: New Harbinger, 1988).

The problem with these thoughts is that they are often negative and can vary in terms of their accuracy. Since these thoughts are not always completely accurate, they may cause us unnecessary distress. When their interpretation of events is extreme or inaccurate we refer to them as "cognitive distortions." We will talk more about how to change these thoughts to be more realistic in later sessions. In this session, we want to focus on becoming aware of these thoughts and how they affect the way we feel.

Awareness of Physical Tension

Just as we may not be aware of our automatic thoughts, we also may not pay attention to how our bodies respond to stress. Bodily signals can be obvious, like a headache after a stressful day at work. Sometimes, though, the signals are more subtle, like changes in the way we are breathing, tension in our muscles, or trouble sleeping for no reason. Becoming aware of these signals alerts us to stress and allows us to "nip it in the bud" as soon as possible. Knowing your sources of stress and how you respond to them physically is an important first step to making changes.

Exercises to Increase Awareness of Physical Symptoms of Stress

The following exercises are designed to introduce you to the concept that your thoughts and emotions directly influence physical sensations in your body. The first exercise helps you to identify where physical tension has built up in your body. The next imagery exercise illustrates the connection between thoughts, emotions, and physical sensations. These exercises are to be first practiced in the group session. Periodically repeating these exercises on your own may help you to identify the extent to which physical stress responses are changing in your body.

Mental Body Scan Exercise

Close your eyes, find yourself in a comfortable position, and start to become aware of how your body feels. Bring your attention from the top of your head slowly down your body until you reach your toes. Become aware of any muscle tension, pressure, tightness or any feelings of pain or discomfort. Focus on areas where tension builds up, such as the abdomen, shoulders, back, and neck. Ask the following questions:

- In what part of my body am I most tight?
- How long has this tension been there?

What is going on that is causing the tension? What stress have I encountered recently? What am I thinking?

Imagery Exercise: Thoughts, Emotions, and Physical Sensations

Close your eyes and think of someone you love or care about a lot. Get a good picture of the person in your mind—her face and expression, the color of her hair and eyes, the kind of clothes she wears, how she holds herself. Imagine how her voice sounds and how she smells. Think about how you feel when you are with her. Become aware of the physical sensations in your body. Pay particular attention to your chest and stomach, where we feel a lot of the sensations that are connected with our emotions. Do you feel tight or loose? Open or closed? Do you feel warm inside or have butterflies? Do you have a rising or sinking feeling? Take in all the sensations of your body and think about how they feel.

RELAXATION TRAINING: *Progressive Muscle Relaxation for Eight Muscle Groups*

Goals

■ To practice PMR for eight muscle groups

PMR for Eight Muscle Groups

Last session you learned the first relaxation procedure, PMR for 16 Muscle Groups. This session continues with the theme of tensing and relaxing but with fewer muscle groups, making the procedure faster and easier to complete.

Follow the same instructions that you used for the PMR for 16 Muscle Groups in Session 1, except use only the following eight muscle groups:

1. Upper and lower arms

2. Upper and lower legs

3. Stomach

4. Chest

5. Shoulders

6. Neck

7. Eyes

8. Forehead (either upper or lower)

Remember, it is important to practice PMR every day (twice a day if possible) in order to gain the most benefit from this relaxation technique.

Homework

✎ Practice PMR for Eight Muscle Groups on a daily basis (twice a day if possible). Record stress levels before and after each practice on the Daily Self-Monitoring Sheet.

✎ Continue to monitor your stress levels at specified times each day and record on the Daily Self-Monitoring Sheet.

✎ For every stressful event that comes up this week, note your automatic thoughts and emotional and physical responses on the Thoughts, Feelings, and Physical Sensations Monitoring Sheet in this chapter. You may photocopy this form from the book or download multiple copies from the Treatments *ThatWork*™ Web site at www.oup.com/us/ttw.

✎ Come up with examples of common everyday situations that cause you stress and record on the Thoughts, Feelings, and Physical Sensations Monitoring Sheet.

✎ Try to be aware of obvious and subtle stress signals during the week and record these on the Thoughts, Feelings, and Physical Sensations Monitoring Sheet.

Thoughts, Feelings, and Physical Sensations Monitoring Sheet

Use this form to record stressful situations and your responses to them.

Situation	Automatic Thoughts	Emotions	Physical Sensations
My boss yelled at me.	He has no right to treat me this way.	anger, frustration	Stomach rumbling, teeth clenched

Chapter 4

Session 3: Linking Thoughts and Emotions /
Breathing, Imagery, Progressive Muscle
Relaxation for Four Muscle Groups

Overview

In the stress management section of this session, you will learn how thoughts, emotions, and physical sensations are interrelated and can create a cycle that can lead to negative outcomes. This program will teach you how to interrupt that cycle at the level of thoughts by changing your "appraisals" of stressful situations. The steps of the appraisal process will be introduced. You will begin practicing the first steps of the appraisal process by becoming aware of your negative thoughts and their relationship to your emotions and physical sensations. The relaxation section will teach a breathing technique to reduce tension and stress. It will also introduce how to use imagery for relaxation. In addition, you will continue with progressive muscle relaxation, but with even fewer muscle groups.

STRESS MANAGEMENT: *Linking Thoughts and Emotions*

Goals

  ▨ To review your home study of previous chapters

  ▨ To explore the relationship between thoughts and feelings

  ▨ To understand the cycle of thoughts, emotions, and physical sensations

  ▨ To begin learning about the appraisal process

Review of Previous Chapters

Before moving on to new material it is helpful to review what you have learned in previous sessions. This will make it easier for you to integrate new information. Review the different effects of stress covered in Session 2 by turning to that section of your workbook. During that session you learned that people may experience cognitive, emotional, behavioral, physical, and social effects of stress. You completed a Symptoms of Stress Checklist to identify which stress symptoms are problems for you. Review your list and think about whether you experienced any of these stress symptoms during the past week. If so, make sure you recorded them on your Thoughts, Feelings, and Physical Sensations Monitoring Sheet for homework.

Relationship Between Thoughts and Feelings

Many people believe that stressful situations are to blame for their distress, discomfort, and misery. However, the events themselves do not cause our stress responses, but rather it is the way we process and think about them that is critical to the way we feel. The same situation may be stressful for one person and not for another, because they think about the situation differently. If you think of HIV infection as a death sentence, then understandably you would feel a lot of stress and may become more anxious or depressed. On the other hand, if you perceive HIV infection as a manageable condition, then you would experience less stress over your status, might be more confident, and would perhaps be more willing to take some positive actions to manage your health. It is not the situation but your *thoughts* about the situation that cause your emotions to be moved in either a positive or negative direction.

Linking Thoughts and Feelings Exercise

Understanding that negative thoughts are the primary cause of negative emotions such as anxiety, anger, and depression is a critical first step in getting your thoughts (and ultimately your emotions) under control. The following exercise illustrates the link between thoughts and emotions. Review the events and the negative thoughts one might have about these situations. For each negative thought in the left column, identify a feeling that would likely result.

Event 1: For the past several weeks your significant other goes out with friends after work and stays out most of the evening.

Thoughts/Self-Talk	Feelings
1. He/she doesn't like my company anymore.	I feel worthless
I am boring. I can't keep anyone interested in me.	
2. He/she must have found someone else.	Hurt and sad
He/she doesn't love me anymore.	
3. He/she is not there when I need him/her the most.	
He/she is a bad person. This is not fair.	
4. He/she has difficulty coping with my illness and doesn't know how to deal with it. I should have been more supportive.	

Event 2: Recently, an additional person has been hired where you work to perform similar duties to yours.

Thoughts/Self-Talk	Feelings
1. I have always been at my best. As soon as I have a health problem they try to replace me. This is not fair.	Furious
2. I am not able to do a very good job anymore. If I was better at my job they wouldn't need anyone else.	
I will never be as good as I was.	

3. They hired someone else because they are thinking of replacing me. If I lose my job, I will end up on the street. _____

4. They think I need help because I can't handle the stress. _____

I should have told them that I was doing well. _____

Thoughts, Emotions, and Physical Sensations

Negative thoughts not only lead to negative emotions, but also affect the way we feel physically. In the group meeting for this session, you practiced a Power of Thought Exercise. This exercise demonstrated how our thoughts can create physical sensations. If you have anxious thoughts, you will probably experience a negative mood and physical stress symptoms.

When you experience unpleasant emotions or uncomfortable physical sensations, these can be a clue that you are having negative thoughts. Use the Thoughts, Feelings, and Physical Sensations Monitoring Sheet to keep track of these feelings and the thoughts and situations they are associated with.

The Appraisal Process

We have seen that the way we think can affect the way we feel. The next step is to take a closer look at our thoughts.

Accurate and Inaccurate Appraisals

Our thoughts can be accurate or inaccurate appraisals (or interpretations) of reality. When our perceptions about an external event are correct and accurate, then our emotions and mood will be appropriate and match the situation. For example, if you really are being fired unfairly, you have a right to be angry. When you have distressing and upsetting emotions, the key is to examine whether these feelings are caused by accurate or inaccurate perceptions of external events. Often, when you experience negative emotions you will find that you are thinking in a distorted or extreme manner.

Steps of the Appraisal Process

The appraisal process includes the following steps.

Step 1: Become Aware of Negative Thinking Patterns

- What negative things are you saying to yourself?

Step 2: Learn to Recognize Anxiety-Producing Appraisals

- How do these negative thoughts make you feel?

Step 3: Begin to Notice That These Thoughts Are Automatic

- Do these thoughts happen so fast they feel automatic?

Step 4: Take Note That These Thoughts Are Often Negative and Distorted

- Are these thoughts accurate or inaccurate perceptions of reality?
- How are these thoughts extreme or distorted?

Step 5: Begin to Change to More Balanced Appraisals

- Can you think of more rational thoughts that will help you cope with the situation?

Example of the Appraisal Process

The following story illustrates how the appraisal process can be used to break the cycle of negative thoughts and feelings.

An individual who lost his job and was seeking new employment found himself quite anxious and depressed before a job interview. He examined his negative thoughts—"I will never get this job; I am not qualified; the people here will never like me"—and found that it was likely he was appraising the situation in an overly negative and unrealistic manner. Thus, he attempted to break his cycle of negative emotion by changing his negative thoughts to something more positive, like "I have an even chance of getting this job; I am well-prepared for this interview; if I don't get this job, there are several other jobs advertised for which I am qualified." These more realistic and accurate thoughts reduced his anxiety and depression levels and helped him to feel more comfortable in the interview.

Step 1: Become Aware of Negative Thinking Patterns

In the preceding example, the interviewee first had to become aware that he was saying something unrealistically negative to himself.

Step 2: Learn to Recognize Anxiety-Producing Appraisals

Next he had to learn to recognize his anxiety-producing appraisals (thoughts about the situation). Negative thoughts like "I am not qualified" were making him feel depressed and anxious.

Step 3: Begin to Notice That These Thoughts Are Automatic

Thoughts like the ones the interviewee had occur so quickly that we refer to them as "automatic." His judgment that "people here will never like me" is not based on an assessment of the situation but on habitual assumptions.

Step 4: Take Note That These Thoughts Are Often Negative and Distorted

The automatic thoughts that are associated with anxiety and other negative emotions are often negative and distorted. For example, the thought "I'll never get this job" is an unrealistic appraisal of the situation, because the employer was impressed enough with the man's résumé to call him for an interview. The employer was willing to consider giving him the job, so he did in fact have some chance.

Step 5: Begin to Change to More Balanced Appraisals

Once the interviewee learned to identify his negative thoughts, he could then work on changing them. With practice, less distorted thoughts (i.e., more balanced appraisals) would become automatic, and the process of identifying and changing unrealistic negative thoughts would also become automatic.

Beneficial Aspects of Negative Thinking

By this point, you may believe that all forms of negative thinking are unnecessary, extreme, and irrational. Nothing could be further from the truth. Quite often, you might experience unpleasant, tragic, and upsetting events in your life that you believe to be negative. As a result of these beliefs, you experience unpleasant emotions. If you are perceiving a situation accurately, your distressing emotions will serve a useful function for you. For example, if a close friend has died and you are extremely sad because you miss your close relationship, crying, grieving, and sadness will allow you to work through the difficult situation and incorporate it into your experience so that you can move on with your life. Only when the thoughts take on an unrealistically negative and distorted quality (e.g., "my life is over because my friend is gone; the same fate will soon befall me; I have nothing left to look forward to in my life") is it likely that you will experience emotions and behavioral reactions that are dysfunctional and self-defeating.

The examples on page 34 help illustrate the potentially useful functions of negative thinking that arise from accurate perceptions of stressful situations.

Take a moment and note how your own recent experiences of sadness, anger, guilt, and anxiety had different self-talk patterns and specific functions. By getting familiar with what these emotions feel like, what behaviors and physical sensations they are accompanied

Feelings	Thoughts/Self-Talk	Function
Sadness	I am very unfortunate. Poor me! I have lost something important. There is nothing I can do.	Prepares and motivates you to grieve and to reinvest in something else
Anger	This is not OK. This is wrong! This is someone else's fault. It should not be like this. I'll show them!	Prepares and motivates you to achieve a goal and remove barriers, or protect yourself
Guilt	I am not okay. I was wrong. I should have done more. Could I have done something to avoid this or can I fix it now?	Motivates you to adhere to personal and social norms
Anxiety	I am in danger! Something bad could happen to me. I'd better get prepared to fight or escape fast.	Prepares and motivates you to meet a challenge to escape danger

by, and in what situations they emerge, you will be better able to understand how thoughts and feelings are linked in your own life.

- Are any of these thoughts particularly familiar to you?

- Do you see both the negative (self-defeating) and positive (functional) aspects of these processes?

- Which emotional experience is a particularly common occurrence in your life?

- When you are under stress or challenged in some way by other people, are you more likely to experience

  - Sadness?

  - Anger?

  - Guilt?

  - Anxiety?

If you experience more than one of these on a regular basis, is one of them more intense than others? For example, are your anxiety experiences fairly mild, while your anger responses are quite explosive? Or are you more likely to experience half-hearted angry feelings but have trouble swimming in heavy guilt feelings for the whole day?

Monitoring and the Appraisal Process

The appraisal process takes a lot of practice to master. In the next couple of sessions, you will spend more time examining your negative thoughts and learning how to change them. For now, focus on becoming more aware of your automatic thoughts and how they make you feel. Keep using the Thoughts, Feelings, and Physical Sensations Monitoring Sheet (see end of chapter 3) to record stressful situations, the automatic thoughts that you have about these situations, and the corresponding emotions and physical symptoms that you experience. You may want to select one stressful event per day to focus your attention on for about 20 minutes. For each one, try to recall your immediate thoughts about the situation and the feelings and sensations that accompanied these thoughts. Sometimes you will recall only the emotional "outcome" of the situation. In time you will train yourself to be more aware of the thoughts (appraisals) that preceded these emotional reactions as well as the accompanying physical sensations.

RELAXATION TRAINING: *Breathing, Imagery, Progressive Muscle Relaxation for Four Muscle Groups*

Goals

- To practice diaphragmatic breathing

- To practice imagery for relaxation

- To practice PMR for Four Muscle Groups

Diaphragmatic Breathing

Diaphragmatic breathing is a valuable and simple tool for stress management. By learning to use the diaphragm, a muscle separating the chest from the abdomen, you can begin taking deeper breaths. This kind of breathing can be seen when a sleeping infant's stomach slowly rises and falls with each breath. Most people rarely use such deep natural breathing in the course of their daily activities. Particularly when we become stressed, the tendency is to breathe much more shallowly in the upper sections of the lungs.

Shallow breathing takes in less oxygen to nourish the body. Toxins are not removed from circulation, resulting in decreased functioning of bodily organs, less energy, and more tension. Deep diaphragmatic breaths, on the other hand, allow greater amounts of oxygen to be available for use by the body. This kind of breathing gives you greater control over physical tension. When you are less tense, you are more able to follow up with more efficient coping strategies.

Diaphragmatic Breathing Exercise

To practice diaphragmatic breathing, get into a comfortable position. Put one hand on your stomach and the other on your chest. Inhale slowly and watch which hand moves. Shallow breaths move the hand on the chest; diaphragmatic breaths move the hand on the stomach. Make sure your breath is moving the hand on the stomach before beginning the diaphragmatic exercise.

To start, slowly inhale through your nose. As you breathe in, count slowly to 4 and feel your stomach expand with your hand. Hold the breath for 4 seconds. Then slowly breathe out while counting to 4. Hold for 4 seconds before taking the next inhale. Keep breathing in this pattern, feeling yourself becoming more relaxed with every exhale:

Breathe in, 1 . . . , 2 . . . , 3 . . . , 4 . . . Hold, 1 . . . , 2 . . . , 3 . . . , 4 . . . Breathe out, 1 . . . , 2 . . . , 3 . . . , 4 . . . . Hold, 1 . . . , 2 . . . , 3 . . . , 4 . . .

Practice this exercise at least two times a day in order to develop good breathing habits. At first you may want to practice when you are relaxed and will not be disturbed. Once you become more skilled, however, you can begin to practice at other places and times during the day. You can practice diaphragmatic breathing in 30-second to 2-minute intervals—for example, while waiting for a red light or an elevator or for someone to answer the phone. Since you have to breathe anyway, no one will even notice you are breathing for relaxation. Using deep breathing during times of stress will help you relax and put you in a better position to respond to the situation.

Relaxation and Imagery

When focusing our attention on pleasant images (e.g., nature scenes, people we love), we generally feel calm, peaceful, and relaxed. Try using imagery to induce relaxation as part of your home practice. Imagine the same scene that you were guided through in session, or come up with your own relaxing scene (e.g., a beach, a meadow, a mountain view). Use whatever images help you to relax. This exercise works best by listening to an audio recording of an imagery script. Use a recording provided by your group leaders or create your own. At first you may have difficulty imagining the scene or becoming relaxed, but with practice this exercise will become easier and more enjoyable.

PMR for Four Muscle Groups

Continue to practice progressive muscle relaxation, but now try practicing with only four muscle groups. At first you may find the shorter exercise a little difficult, but with practice you will be able to tense and relax just as well. The four recommended muscle groups are:

1. Stomach

2. Chest

3. Shoulders

4. Forehead (either upper or lower)

If you experience a lot of tension in another muscle group, you may want to substitute or add it to your practice. It is important that you practice every day in preparation for next session's passive relaxation exercise, which will use these four muscle groups.

Homework

✎ Practice PMR for Four Muscle Groups on a daily basis (twice a day if possible). Record stress levels before and after each practice on the Daily Self-Monitoring Sheet.

✎ Practice diaphragmatic breathing on a daily basis and record stress levels before and after on the Daily Self-Monitoring Sheet.

✎ Perform the imagery exercise at least once a day and record stress levels before and after on the Daily Self-Monitoring Sheet.

✎ Continue to monitor your stress levels at specified times each day and record on the Daily Self-Monitoring Sheet.

✎ Review the Linking Thoughts and Feelings Exercise in this chapter.

✎ Complete the Thoughts, Feelings, and Physical Sensations Monitoring Sheet (see end of Chapter 3) for every stressful event this week. You may want to select one stressful event per day to focus your attention on for about 20 minutes.

Chapter 5

Session 4: Negative Thinking and Cognitive Distortions / Breathing, Imagery, Passive Progressive Muscle Relaxation

Overview

This session introduces common types of negative thinking and cognitive distortions. You will practice identifying negative thoughts and labeling the type of distortion. For relaxation, you will learn how to combine imagery with diaphragmatic breathing. You will also practice passive PMR, in which you simply remember the feeling of tension instead of actually tensing the muscles. Passive PMR will be immediately followed by a special place imagery exercise.

STRESS MANAGEMENT: *Negative Thinking and Cognitive Distortions*

Goals

- To examine the different types of negative thinking and cognitive distortions

- To practice identifying negative thoughts

- To understand the effect of negative thinking on behavior

Examples of Negative Thinking and Cognitive Distortions

As we discussed in the last session, sometimes negative thinking reflects an accurate perception of reality, and in this case it can help us take appropriate action. Sometimes, however, our negative thoughts are inaccurate or distorted appraisals of the situation. This causes us to experience distress unnecessarily.

This session introduces some of the most common types of negative thinking or cognitive distortions. These are adapted from D. Burns, *Feeling Good: The New Mood Therapy* (New York: New American Library, 1981) to apply to some of the challenges that face persons with HIV.

All-or-Nothing Thinking (Black-and-White Thinking)

You think in black and white terms; there are no in-betweens or gray areas. Perfectionism is often the result of this kind of thinking. You are afraid to make any mistakes, because if you are not perfect then you see yourself as a complete failure. This type of thinking is unrealistic because things are rarely all good or all bad. Examples of this kind of thinking are, "If you're not 100% supportive, then you're against me" or "I can't cope with any of my new medications; I can't do anything right."

Overgeneralization

You see a single negative event as part of a pattern of defeat. You conclude that something that happened to you once will occur over and over again. For example, suppose your partner just broke up with you. You might think, "This relationship didn't work; I'll never be in a good relationship. Nobody will ever want me; I'll always be lonely and alone."

Mental Filter

You pick out a single negative detail and focus on it so much that you can't see anything positive. When you are depressed you see the world through special glasses that darken your entire view of reality. Only the negative things get through and since you don't realize that you are filtering out the positive, you assume that there is nothing positive and everything really is negative. For example, you have a review at work and your boss gives you some criticism as well as praise. Afterwards, the only thing you can think about is the criticism.

Disqualifying the Positive

You discount any positive experiences and so keep believing that things are completely negative. This kind of thinking is very harmful, since you cannot be convinced that you have any value no matter what happens. For example, if people want to spend time with you, you think, "They just feel sorry for me because I have HIV."

Jumping to Conclusions

In the absence of solid evidence, you jump to a negative conclusion. There are two types of this: "mind reading" and the "fortune teller error."

Mind Reading

You assume that you know what someone else is thinking. You are so convinced that someone is having a negative reaction to you, you don't even take the time to confirm your guess. For example, you see an acquaintance at a party and she doesn't come over to talk. You think, "She's avoiding me because she knows I have HIV." It's possible, however, that she was just caught up in conversation with someone else.

The Fortune Teller Error

You act as a fortune teller who only predicts the worst for you. You then treat your prediction as if it were a proven fact. For example, you think, "Since I'm HIV-infected, I'm going to die real soon," versus "I don't know how long it's going to be and there are plenty of things I can do in the meantime."

Magnification (Catastrophizing) or Minimization

You magnify the importance of negative things (e.g., errors you made at work) and minimize the significance of positive things (e.g., your own accomplishments). It's as if you are looking through either the small or large end of binoculars.

An example of magnification is, "I made a mistake at work. Now everyone will know and my reputation will be ruined!" You are catastrophizing your mistakes as if you were looking through binoculars that make them look larger than they really are.

Minimization occurs when you look at your strengths and good points and minimize their significance as if you were looking through the wrong end of the binoculars. For example, you think, "I did a good job, but it's not a big deal. Anyone could have done it" or "My T-cells increased by 50 since this new medication started, but I still have 100 less T cells than last year at this time."

Emotional Reasoning

You let your negative emotions convince you that how you feel is the way things really are. For example: "I feel guilty, therefore I deserve this" or "I feel depressed, therefore I'm a loser." Since your feelings reflect your thoughts and beliefs, which may be distorted, these emotions may have little validity. Emotional reasoning plays a role in keeping some people depressed; things *feel* so negative they assume they truly are.

"Should" Statements

You try to motivate yourself with "shoulds," "musts," and "oughts" as if you had to be reprimanded before you could be expected to do anything. Guilt is the result of this kind of thinking. When you use these statements toward others, it can cause you to feel anger, frustration, and resentment. Common examples are, "I must be able to handle my condition all by myself" or "I should not ask for help" or "If people care about me, they ought to be able to tell I need help with managing all these medications."

Labeling and Mislabeling

Personal labeling means creating a completely negative self-image based on one mistake. Instead of describing your actions ("I did something stupid") you attach a negative label to yourself ("I'm stupid"). When someone else's behavior bothers you, you attach a negative label to him: "He's a jerk." Mislabeling involves describing an event with language that is emotionally extreme. For example: "The meeting was a total waste of time" or "All the time I spent exercising this month was a wash since I still gained a pound."

Personalization

You see yourself as the cause of some negative external event for which in fact you were not primarily responsible. You arbitrarily decide that a negative occurrence is your fault or reflects your inadequacy. Personalization causes you to feel guilt: "My lover is depressed, and it's my fault," "My viral load went up this week and I caused it."

Labeling Cognitive Distortions and Corresponding Emotions Exercise

Try to identify the type of distortion associated with each of the following thoughts.

1. Someone is starting to experience cold symptoms. He thinks, "I must have PCP [Pneumocystis pneumonia]. I probably only have a week to live."

   Cognitive Distortion: _____

2. Ahead of you, you see an acquaintance on the street walking your way. He passes without saying hello. You say to yourself, "He must be angry with me."

   Cognitive Distortion: _____

3. For the past several weeks your lover has gone out with friends after work and stayed out most of the night. You think, "He must have found someone else; he doesn't love me anymore. I can't keep anyone interested in me; this always happens to me."

   Cognitive Distortion: _____

4. Recently an additional person has been hired to perform duties similar to yours. You say to yourself, "I am being replaced; if I

lose my job I'll end up on the street; if I was any good at my job, they wouldn't need anyone else."

Cognitive Distortion: _____

Now, try to think of some personal examples of distorted thinking as related to the following:

1. Family relationships

   Event: _____

   Thought: _____

   Cognitive Distortion: _____

2. Receiving T-cell count or viral load results

   Event: _____

   Thought: _____

   Cognitive Distortion: _____

3. Quality of healthcare

   Event: _____

   Thought: _____

   Cognitive Distortion: _____

4. Support network

   Event: _____

   Thought: _____

   Cognitive Distortion: _____

Negative Thoughts and Behaviors

Negative thoughts affect not only the way we feel but also the way we behave and how we, in turn, trigger reactions in others. For example, if we have thoughts that we are unwanted, we may withdraw from a relationship; if we think someone is out to get us, we might launch a preemptive attack against her. This type of self-defeating behavior pattern may act as a self-fulfilling prophecy (when the other person appraises our actions and responds with the behaviors we were expecting). This can set off a negative interaction in a relationship when there wasn't one in the first place.

We may also smoke, drink, or use drugs to deal with our painful emotions. We may even try to deny that problems exist in order to avoid dealing with them. Chronic use of these kind of behaviors often causes the problems to grow bigger, creating more stress and leading us to engage in even more negative thinking and cognitive distortions. Identifying negative thought patterns is the first step in breaking this vicious cycle of thoughts, behaviors, and stress.

RELAXATION TRAINING: *Breathing, Imagery, Passive Progressive Muscle Relaxation*

Goals

- To combine diaphragmatic breathing with imagery
- To practice passive PMR with special place imagery

Diaphragmatic Breathing with Imagery

Remember, with diaphragmatic breathing you breathe in to the count of 4, hold to the count of 4, exhale to the count of 4, and hold to the count of 4.

Breathe in, 1 . . . , 2 . . . , 3 . . . , 4 . . . Hold, 1 . . . , 2 . . . , 3 . . . , 4 . . . Breathe out, 1 . . . , 2 . . . , 3 . . . , 4 . . . . Hold, 1 . . . , 2 . . . , 3 . . . , 4 . . .

You can enhance your practice of diaphragmatic breathing by using imagery. As you did in session, lie down in a relaxed position. Place your hands gently on your abdomen and continue diaphragmatic breathing to the count of 4.

Imagine that, with each breath of air coming in, energy is coming into your lungs. As you hold, energy is being stored in the center of your body and flowing out to all parts of your body. Imagine that as you exhale, any tension is leaving your body. Form a picture of this in your mind, breathing in and letting energy come into your body, holding, and letting the energy flow through your body. Breathe out, letting go of any tension, and hold, letting yourself remain in a clear, calm, state. Breathe quietly for a few minutes, then gradually bring yourself back to awareness and open your eyes.

Passive PMR with Imagery

In this exercise, you will recall the relaxation of doing PMR using four muscle groups while imagining a safe, secure place. You will use the same four muscle groups that you used in the last session (stomach, chest, shoulders, forehead), but this time you will no longer actually tense the muscles but instead will simply remember what that tension felt like. After recalling the feelings of tension, completely relax that muscle group.

Practice the passive PMR for Four Muscle Groups, and then without stopping move into imagining your special place. This allows you to experience the benefits of both procedures in the same relaxation session.

Special Place Imagery

Think of a special place—a place you have been or have seen in a movie or a picture, or an imaginary place—where you feel calm and safe.

Begin the exercise by focusing on your breathing. Feel yourself breathing, deeper and deeper, slower and slower, becoming more and more relaxed with every breath. As you breathe in you can mentally say to yourself a word like "relax" or any phrase that will help you just let go and bring yourself to a deeper state of calm and peace. As you breathe out, you can let go of all your tension, all your stress. If you notice thoughts going by, it's okay. Just notice them as they drift by.

As you are feeling completely relaxed, imagine a place, a special place that you enjoy, where you feel peaceful, calm, and relaxed. Let yourself be in that place now. Look around you. See the shapes and colors of your special place. Be aware of all the sensations in your special place. Breathe in, and as you breathe in, let yourself be completely filled with the serenity of this special place. Allow yourself to experience its beauty. Let it nourish and calm you. Go over these different sensations again, allowing yourself to become more and more relaxed.

Breathe in the calm deeper and deeper, letting it fill you. Know that this is a place you always have inside of you and that you have the ability to go there any time you want by breathing deeply in and out, gently closing your eyes, and taking yourself to this inner healing place.

To come out of the exercise, count from 1 to 4. Gradually begin to move your body, and then open your eyes and come to a fully alert state.

Homework

✎ Practice diaphragmatic breathing with imagery on a daily basis (twice a day if possible). Record stress levels before and after each practice on the Daily Self-Monitoring Sheet.

✎ Practice passive PMR with special place imagery on a daily basis (twice a day if possible). Record stress levels before and after each practice on the Daily Self-Monitoring Sheet.

✎ Continue to monitor your stress levels at specified times each day and record on the Daily Self-Monitoring Sheet.

✎ Complete the Labeling Cognitive Distortions and Corresponding Emotions Exercise in this chapter.

✎ Complete the Stress Responses and Types of Negative Thoughts Monitoring Sheet to identify the types of negative thinking associated with your stressful situations this week. Make sure to also record your corresponding emotions and physical symptoms. You may photocopy this form from the book or download multiple copies from the Treatments *That-Work*™ Web site at www.oup.com/us/ttw.

Stress Responses and Types of Negative Thoughts Monitoring Sheet

Use this form to record stressful situations and your responses to them. Label your automatic thoughts with the type of negative thinking being used.

Situation	Automatic Thoughts	Type of Negative Thinking	Emotions (Rate intensity on a scale of 1 to 4; 1 = low, 4 = high)	Physical Symptoms
Mess up an important assignment at work	I'm an idiot. I'm going to get fired.	Labeling Jumping to conclusions	depressed = 3 anxious = 4	headache, neck muscles tightened

Chapter 6

Session 5: Rational Thought Replacement /
Autogenic Training for Heaviness and Warmth

Overview

The stress management portion of this session focuses on replacing irrational thoughts with rational thoughts. First, you must understand the difference between irrational and rational self-talk and be able to identify each. You will then learn and practice the five steps of rational thought replacement. This session also discusses the importance of relaxation for stress management. You will learn a new relaxation technique, autogenic training, and practice inducing heaviness and warmth in your body.

STRESS MANAGEMENT: *Rational Thought Replacement*

Goals

- To identify irrational and rational self-talk

- To learn the steps to rational thought replacement

- To practice replacing distorted thoughts with rational thoughts

Differences Between Irrational and Rational Self-Talk

As discussed in the last session, the thoughts that we have in response to stressful situations may reflect whether we have perceived a situation accurately or inaccurately. When we appraise a situation correctly, our thoughts are generally rational, realistic, and appropriate for the situation. In contrast, inaccurate perceptions of stressful situations are irrational, unrealistic, and extreme.

Rational self-talk reflects appropriate concern for the difficulties that we face, demonstrating a balanced perception of reality:

- *This is a difficult situation, but there are things I can do to improve it.*

- *I can't change the fact that I have HIV, but I can manage my condition.*

Irrational self-talk often leads us to either deny that problems exist or blow the magnitude of problems far out of proportion:

- *It's not really a problem. I'll just ignore it.*

- *This is a catastrophe! There's nothing I can do to fix it.*

Irrational self-talk often keeps us from dealing directly with our problems, causing them to build until they are out of control. Irrational self-talk is based on cognitive distortions that often cause emotional and physical distress. By changing distorted negative thinking patterns we can relieve unnecessary distress. The goal is to change distorted thoughts so that they reflect accurate perceptions of reality while still showing appropriate concern over the stressors.

Identifying Irrational and Rational Self-Talk Exercise

For the following situation, identify the corresponding statements as irrational or rational. Write your answer in the blank provided.

Situation: You are running short on cash this week. You have a friend who owes you $50. You have left several phone messages telling him that you want him to repay you before the weekend. He has not returned your calls. The following thoughts go through your head:

1. *My friend is worthless. He is just using me.*

   Type of Self-Talk: _____

2. *I was so dumb to lend him money. I should have known I would need it.*

   Type of Self-Talk: _____

3. *I guess it's okay if I don't get the money; I don't need to eat this week.*

   Type of Self-Talk: _____

4. *I will continue to pursue the matter with him. The next time a friend asks for a loan, I will discuss repayment before I give him the money.*

   Type of Self-Talk: _____

Steps to Rational Thought Replacement

You can take steps to change your negative thought processes so that they are more in line with reality. By replacing your irrational thoughts with more rational ones, you may improve your emotional and physical well-being. The five steps (A, B, C, D, E) to rational thought replacement are outlined as follows.

Step A: Become AWARE: Identify Self-Talk

- Focus on what you are thinking about yourself, the other person, or the situation

- Identify automatic thoughts that are negative and possibly inaccurate

- Identify the feelings and behaviors related to the self-talk

Step B: Rate Your BELIEF in Each Negative Thought

Select a negative thought, and rate (0–100%) the extent to which you believed that thought was true at the time when you were thinking it. If you were completely convinced that the thought was true, rate it 100%. If you believed that there was no truth to the thought, then rate it 0%.

Step C: CHALLENGE Yourself: Dispute Negative Self-Talk

Select a negative thought and challenge it with the following questions:

- "What actual support is there for this idea?"

- "What evidence exists that this idea is false?"

- "What is the worst thing that could happen to me?"

    - "How bad is that worst thing?"

    - "How likely is that outcome?"

    - "How could I handle the worst case scenario?"

- "What good things might occur? How likely are they to happen?"

Step D: DISCARD the Distortion: Change the Negative Thought to a More Rational One

Use the following questions to help to discard negative thoughts and replace them with rational responses:

- "What can I say to myself that will reduce excessive negative feelings?"

- "What can I say to myself that will be self-enhancing instead of a put-down?"

- "What can I say to myself that will help me cope with the situation appropriately?"

- "How do I want to feel and act in this situation?"

- "What do I need to say to myself that will help bring that about?"

Then rate your belief in your rational responses on a scale of 0% to 100%.

Step E: EVALUATE the Outcome

The last step is to evaluate the outcome of changing negative thinking. First, re-rate your belief in your automatic negative thoughts on a scale of 0% to 100%. Then specify and rate (0–100%) the emotions associated with those thoughts.

Use the Rational Thought Replacement Sheet on page 54 to practice these steps. You may photocopy this form from the workbook or download multiple copies from the Treatments *ThatWork*™ Web site at www.oup.com/us/ttw.

Generating Rational Responses

Probably the most difficult aspect of rational thought replacement for many people involves generating rational responses that are genuine and believable. If you find it difficult to generate rational responses, try using the following examples as an initial response to inaccurate self-talk. These examples can be expanded upon by creating additional rational thoughts appropriate for the situation.

- "I may feel a negative emotion, but the situation itself doesn't do anything to me"

- "Nobody's perfect"

- "It takes two to have a conflict"

- "We can influence how we feel by the way we think"

Helpful Guidelines for Generating Rational Responses

- Pick specific thoughts to refute and replace

- Deal with specific problems, not with general philosophical stances

- If you get stuck and can't think of a rational response, come back to it

- Think of how someone else would respond

Rational Thought Replacement Sheet

Step A: Become AWARE: Identify Self-Talk

1. Identify a self-statement that is inaccurate or negative: _____

2. Identify feelings and behaviors related to this thought: _____

Step B: Rate Your BELIEF in the Negative Thought

Rate the extent (0–100%) to which you believed the thought was true at the time when you were thinking it. Belief Rating: _____

Step C: CHALLENGE Yourself: Dispute the Negative Self-Talk

1. What actual support is there for this idea?

_____

2. What evidence exists that this idea is false?

_____

3. What is the worst thing that could happen to me?

_____

4. What good things might occur?

_____

Step D: Discard the DISTORTION: Change the Negative Thought to a More Rational One

1. What can I say to myself that will reduce excessive negative feelings and help me to cope with the situation appropriately?

_____

2. How do I want to feel and act in this situation? What do I need to say to myself that will help bring that about?

_____

Rate your belief in your rational responses (0–100%) 1. _____   2. _____

Step E: EVALUATE the Outcome

Re-rate your belief in your negative self-talk (0–100%) _____

Specify and rate the emotions associated with that self-talk (0–100%)

Emotion _____   Rating _____   Emotion _____   Rating _____

- Think of how you would respond to someone else in the same situation

- Ask someone else how he or she would respond

- Identify flag words in your thinking such as "always," "never," "should," "can't"

- Learn to describe events in less extreme terms: use terms such as "inconvenient," "disappointing," "frustrating," or "well-done" as opposed to "terrible," "horrible," "catastrophic," or "perfect"

RELAXATION TRAINING: *Autogenic Training for Heaviness and Warmth*

Goals

- To integrate relaxation and stress management

- To learn about autogenic training

- To practice autogenic exercise for heaviness and warmth

Integration of Relaxation with Stress Management

Relaxation helps with stress management in a number of ways. It can make you more aware of how you hold tension and whether you are experiencing negative emotions. You can also use relaxation for several purposes:

Prevention

Relaxation can be used in anticipation of a tension-arousing situation. It may prevent you from becoming anxious and distracted.

Preparation

Relaxation can help carry out a challenging coping response. It can prepare you to deal with problems or handle long-term stressors by giving you the mental energy to be flexible and creative in using different strategies.

Recovering

Relaxation can be used to help you recover from an overwhelming situation. It can help you get back on track after you have resolved the situation.

Introduction to Autogenic Training

Autogenic training is a powerful and well-researched method of relaxation based on the research of Oskar Vogt and Johannes Schultz, two physicians living in Berlin around the turn of the 20th century. Vogt found that he was able to teach individuals to induce a state of deep relaxation in themselves with auto(self)-suggestions. Schultz found that self-suggestions inducing heaviness and warmth could also induce a state of deep relaxation very similar to a hypnotic trance. Applying his knowledge of yoga, hypnosis, and self-suggestion, Schultz developed the autogenic method for people wishing to achieve deep relaxation through self-suggestion without reliance on a hypnotist.

Autogenic training includes six standard exercises to be done in a specific sequence. These exercises deal with helping the body to relax and restoring a state of balance following the "fight-or-flight" stress response. Advanced exercises are designed to help focus the mind and to address specific problems. Exercises involve focusing attention on specific parts of the body, repeating specific phrases, and then passively allowing the body to respond rather than forcing any particular desired response. The first standard exercise uses the theme of heaviness. The second exercise induces sensations of warmth. The third exercise directs the attention to balancing cardiac activity. The fourth exercise allows breathing to become regular and natural, the fifth exercise relaxes the abdomen, and the sixth exercise relaxes the muscles of the face and forehead.

Autogenic training involves repeating simple verbal phrases or formulas such as, "My right arm is heavy . . . My right arm is warm." When you repeat a formula, say it slowly, concentrating on the part of the body you are describing, and then pause for a few seconds when you are finished. Each formula should be repeated three times. If you are right-handed, start with your right arm and then proceed to your left arm. If you are left-handed, do the opposite.

Imagery

If you have difficulty feeling a sense of heaviness, try using a visual image of weights or bags of sand attached to your arms and legs. To help induce warmth, imagine lying on a beach with the sun pouring over your body, or imagine your blood vessels opening up and warm blood flowing out to your fingertips and toes.

Passive Concentration

As you do these exercises, allow yourself to experience whatever feelings and sensations come without judgment or expectations. Be aware of your physical sensations, but do not analyze them or try to force them in any particular direction. This observant attitude is often called passive concentration or "witnessing." It is like the attention we use when we watch a movie—we just watch what's on the screen.

Preparation for Practice

When you first practice autogenics, choose a time and place that you will not be disturbed. After you are skilled at achieving a state of relaxation, it will be easier to practice relaxation in other locations and shorter time periods—for example, while waiting for a phone call or for an elevator.

Since this program's autogenic training progresses at a more rapid pace than is traditionally used, it is important for you to practice quite regularly. Begin with 2-minute sessions two times a day.

These exercises are best done before meals—for example, in the afternoon before dinner, or in the morning before breakfast. For your home practice, keep the temperature at a comfortable level and wear comfortable clothes.

If you feel increased anxiety or restlessness during or after the exercises or experience disturbing side effects such as lightheadedness from decreased blood pressure, go back to practicing progressive muscle relaxation exercises instead.

When you are ready to stop a session, say to yourself, "When I open my eyes, I will feel refreshed and alert." Then open your eyes and breathe a few deep breaths as you stretch and flex your arms. Be sure that you are in an alert state when you go on to your regular activities. OK, ready to begin?

Heaviness and Warmth Autogenic Exercise

Before the exercise, get into a comfortable position, either sitting or lying down. Keep your head supported, legs about eight inches apart, toes pointed slightly outward, and arms resting comfortably at your sides without touching them. Close your eyes.

Begin by saying to yourself, "I am completely relaxed and at peace." Repeat this phrase slowly three times while breathing deeply. Continue breathing deeply throughout the exercise, releasing tension with every exhale.

Say each heaviness phrase to yourself three times, feeling that part of your body become heavier with each repetition of the phrase. Concentrate on the feeling of heaviness as you become more and more relaxed. Then repeat the sequence feeling warmth.

1. My right arm is heavy/warm.

2. My left arm is heavy/warm.

3. Both of my arms are heavy/warm.

4. My arms and legs are heavy/warm.

5. My neck and shoulders are heavy/warm.

To end the exercise, say to yourself three times, "I am relaxed and alert." Inhale deeply and exhale, letting go of any remaining tension. When you are ready, slowly open your eyes.

Homework

✎ Choose any of the types of relaxation taught so far in the program (i.e., PMR, breathing, imagery, autogenic training). Practice twice a day and record stress levels before and after on the Daily Self-Monitoring Sheet.

✎ Continue to monitor your stress levels at specified times each day and record on the Daily Self-Monitoring Sheet.

✎ Review the Identifying Irrational and Rational Self-Talk Exercise in this chapter.

✎ Continue to use the Stress Responses and Types of Negative Thoughts Monitoring Sheet (from Session 4).

✎ Complete Rational Thought Replacement Sheets for three separate stressful situations.

✎ Complete the Situations This Week that I Will Have to Cope With worksheet.

Situations This Week That I Will Have to Cope With:

Chapter 7

Session 6: Productive Coping / Autogenic Training for Heartbeat, Breathing, Abdomen, and Forehead

Overview

The stress management section begins with a discussion of how you are using the techniques you've learned in your daily life. It then defines "coping" and presents productive and nonproductive coping strategies. You will learn how coping can be problem-focused or emotion-focused and the best type of coping for different kinds of stressors. You will then identify your own coping style to see how it can be improved. For relaxation, you will continue with autogenic training, adding exercises for heartbeat, breathing, abdomen, and forehead.

STRESS MANAGEMENT: *Productive Coping*

Goals

- To integrate stress management into your daily life
- To understand the definition of coping
- To learn about the types of coping
- To identify your coping style

Skills Self-Check

Take a few moments to think about how you have integrated stress management and relaxation practice into your lifestyle by answering the following questions:

1. How do you find you are using stress management and relaxation techniques?

_____

_____

2. Does breathing and relaxation give you time to come up with more rational appraisals? If not, why?

_____

_____

3. When are these techniques not working?

_____

_____

4. When could you be using these techniques that you're not?

_____

_____

Remember, practice is key to your success. Make sure that you are doing relaxation exercises regularly and completing the stress management monitoring forms for stressful events as they occur during the week. Keep in mind that relaxation and cognitive techniques enhance one another. Feeling relaxed can help you be more open to learning new ways to deal with your stress.

Definition of Coping

The term "coping" is often used in relation to dealing with stressful situations, but it may have different meanings for different people. Think of how you use the word "coping." Do you use it to convey a negative experience that you can do nothing about but put up with (e.g., "I just coped with it")? Or do you use it to express your ability to handle a difficult situation (e.g., "The situation is bad, but fortunately I am able to cope with it")? In this program, we focus on the definition of coping that refers to an individual's efforts to manage demands that are appraised as exceeding her resources. You can cope with overwhelming demands by either changing the way you think about the situation or changing how you behave in the situation.

Types of Productive Coping

Productive coping is adaptive and efficient. It can be problem-focused or emotion-focused.

Problem-Focused Coping

Problem-focused coping involves changing a problem that is causing distress.

Examples of problem-focused coping include:

- Cognitive problem solving
- Decision making
- Conflict resolution
- Seeking information
- Seeking advice
- Goal setting

Problem-focused coping is particularly useful when a stressor is *controllable,* meaning that taking concrete steps to change the stressor can either reduce or eliminate its intensity. For example, one's perception that life is over because one is infected with HIV can be changed for the better by seeking information about medical treatments available.

Emotion-Focused Coping

Emotion-focused coping involves regulating the emotional response produced by a stressful situation. Examples of emotion-focused coping include:

- Cognitive restructuring (e.g., rational thought replacement)
- Emotional expression (e.g., sharing your frustration or fears with someone you trust)

- Behavioral changes (e.g., engaging in pleasant activities)
- Physical stress reduction (e.g., exercising, relaxation, deep breathing)

Emotion-focused coping is most useful when a stressor is *uncontrollable*, meaning that it is beyond our capacity to change or alter. For example, while there is nothing you can do to change the fact that you are HIV-infected, there are techniques you can use to change how you feel about it.

Combining Problem-Focused and Emotion-Focused Coping

Combining problem-focused and emotion-focused coping strategies can be very effective. For example, practicing relaxation (an emotion-focused technique) before a doctor's visit can decrease anxiety. This can help you focus better on information presented by the doctor and make a calm, informed treatment choice (a problem-focused technique).

Using productive coping during periods of high stress can help you feel better emotionally and physically. How you cope with situations is the part of the stress response that is easiest for you to observe and ultimately change. Start to pay attention to the coping strategies you use in everyday life and think of ways you can use problem-focused and emotion-focused coping.

Stress Awareness, Cognitive Appraisals, and Coping Responses

The model in figure 7.1 illustrates the chain of events for stress management.

As discussed, it is important to determine which aspects of a situation are controllable and which are uncontrollable and choose a coping response that matches the stressor—problem-focused behaviors for changeable aspects and emotion-focused strategies for unchangeable aspects. Picking a strategy that doesn't fit with the situation can be counterproductive. For example, trying to change a frustrating situation that is uncontrollable (that is, it cannot be changed) can cause you to become even more distressed.

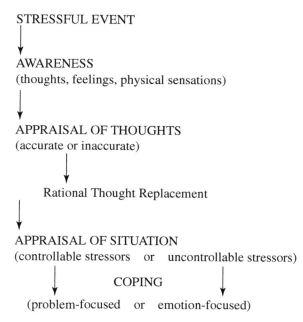

STRESSFUL EVENT

↓

AWARENESS
(thoughts, feelings, physical sensations)

↓

APPRAISAL OF THOUGHTS
(accurate or inaccurate)

↓

Rational Thought Replacement

↓

APPRAISAL OF SITUATION
(controllable stressors   or   uncontrollable stressors)

↓   COPING   ↓

(problem-focused   or   emotion-focused)

Figure 7.1

Model of awareness, appraisal, and coping

Types of Nonproductive Coping

Nonproductive coping strategies are often indirect and less effective. They can be problem-focused or emotion-focused. They usually are automatic reactions or habitual behaviors we have developed over time. By becoming more aware of these nonproductive strategies, you can begin to replace them with more productive strategies.

Nonproductive Problem-Focused Strategies

These actions involve indirectly approaching the problem. Typically the difficulty is dealt with by forms of avoidance.

Behavioral Avoidance: You may go to great lengths in order to avoid a person, place, or activity that makes you uncomfortable.

Cognitive Avoidance: You may distract yourself or even outright deny the problem at hand.

Nonproductive Emotion-Focused Strategies

Nonproductive emotion-focused strategies tend to focus on using less healthy ways of relieving negative emotions. These unhealthy behaviors or thoughts, however, often make emotional difficulties worse. These strategies include:

Consummatory Activities: smoking, eating, and alcohol and recreational drug use/abuse

Feeling Helpless or Hopeless: thoughts that convey an attitude of "giving up"

Engaging in Risky Behaviors: for example, having unprotected sex

Stuffing Feelings Inside: not expressing your emotions; keeping them "bottled up"

Interrelation of Nonproductive Strategies

The use of nonproductive problem-focused strategies often gives rise to the use of nonproductive emotion-focused strategies and vice versa. For example, since avoidance doesn't fix the problem but may make it worse, you then turn to food or alcohol to deal with your anxiety.

Use of nonproductive strategies may make you less likely to confront the problem because they:

▓ Provide temporary relief of irritation or anxiety

▓ Reward you (with food, etc.) for escaping from the problem

▓ Take the "wind out of your sail" and decrease your self-confidence, making you more likely to avoid dealing directly with problems in the future

▓ Perpetuate feelings of helplessness, increasing the likelihood that you may become depressed

Not only are indirect strategies ineffective for dealing with present problems, but they may actually increase depressed feelings. Mood states such as depression are associated with poorer functioning of bodily systems such as the immune system.

Table 7.1 Coping Strategies

	Productive	Nonproductive
Problem-Focused	Problem Solving Decision Making Conflict Resolution Seeking Information Goal Setting Seeking Advice	Behavioral Avoidance Cognitive Avoidance/Denial
Emotion-Focused	Cognitive Restructuring Emotional Expression Relaxation Engaging in Pleasant Activities	Consummatory Activities Feeling Helpless or Hopeless Engaging in Risky Behaviors Stuffing Feelings Inside

Identifying Your Coping Strategies

Refer to table 7.1 to help you identify the coping strategies you often use in both general situations and HIV-related situations. Note these on the My Coping Style worksheet on page 68. Also use the Coping Response Monitoring Sheet at the end of the chapter to record your coping responses for the week.

RELAXATION TRAINING: *Autogenic Training for Heartbeat, Breathing, Abdomen, and Forehead*

Goals

- To learn autogenic formulas for heartbeat, breathing, abdomen, and forehead

- To practice the entire series of autogenic exercises

My Coping Style

What are my most common coping strategies?	Productive	Nonproductive
Problem-focused		
Emotion-focused		

When do I use these strategies?	Productive	Nonproductive
General Situations		
HIV-related Situations		

Autogenic Training

Last session you learned autogenic formulas for heaviness and warmth.

This session introduces sets of instruction for heartbeat, breathing, abdomen, and forehead. You will use the same procedure as described in Session 5, but add new phrases to complete the autogenic series.

Autogenic Exercises for Heartbeat, Abdomen, and Forehead

Repeat the Heaviness and Warmth Autogenic Exercise from Session 5. After completing all the phrases, ending with neck and shoulders, repeat the following phrases three times:

1. "My heartbeat is calm and steady." (If you experience any discomfort, change the phrase to "I am calm and relaxed.")

2. "My breathing is slow and steady."

3. "My abdomen is warm." (If you have abdominal distress, change the phrase to "I am calm and relaxed.")

4. "My forehead is cool and calm."

As you repeat these phrases, breathe deeply, releasing any tension. Feel yourself becoming more and more relaxed with each exhalation of the breath. To complete the series, say to yourself three times, "I am relaxed and alert" and slowly open your eyes. Try to take the feeling of calm and relaxation with you into your day. As you continue to practice autogenic training, you will be able to relax more quickly and more deeply.

Homework

✎ Choose any of the types of relaxation taught so far in the program (i.e., PMR, breathing, imagery, autogenic training). Practice twice a day and record stress levels before and after on the Daily Self-Monitoring Sheet.

✎ Continue to monitor your stress levels at specified times each day and record on the Daily Self-Monitoring Sheet.

✎ Complete the Skills Self-Check in this chapter.

✎ Complete the My Coping Style worksheet in this chapter.

✎ Complete the Coping Response Monitoring Sheet for stressful situations you have to deal with this week. You may photocopy this form from the book or download multiple copies from the Treatments *ThatWork*™ Web site at www.oup.com/us/ttw.

Coping Response Monitoring Sheet

Use this form to record situations that you have to cope with. Practice replacing your automatic thoughts with more rational thoughts. Record your coping behavior and label the type of strategy used (productive or nonproductive; problem-focused or emotion-focused).

Situation	Automatic Thoughts	Rational Thought Replacement	Coping Behavior	Label of Coping Strategy
I had a fight with a friend.	He hates me now. Our friendship is over.	We're good friends. We can probably make up.	I talked things over with him.	Productive, problem-focused

Chapter 8

Session 7: Executing Effective Coping Responses / Autogenic Training with Imagery and Self-Suggestions

Overview

The stress management section of this session introduces the steps for a productive coping plan. You will practice breaking down general situations into specific aspects and choosing appropriate coping strategies. You will also learn a softening technique to help you accept stressful circumstances. The relaxation section builds on the autogenic training from the previous sessions. You will practice autogenics with imagery and self-suggestions to deepen your relaxation.

STRESS MANAGEMENT: *Executing Effective Coping Responses*

Goals

- To learn and practice steps to effective coping
- To practice a softening technique for overwhelming stressors

Steps to Effective Coping

Last session, you learned about productive and nonproductive coping strategies. Review table 7.1 on types of coping in Session 6. Remember that coping behaviors can be problem-focused or emotion-focused. Within productive coping strategies, problem-focused coping is generally most useful for dealing with controllable stressors, and emotion-focused coping is most helpful for handling stressors that seem uncontrollable and unmanageable.

Now that you are familiar with the various types of coping strategies, you can work on using more productive strategies in your daily life. A productive plan of coping includes the following steps:

Step 1. Break down the stressor into specific situations. It is easier to deal with a specific situation (e.g., a report due) rather than a general state of affairs (e.g., a demanding job).

Step 2. Identify specific demands of the situation (e.g., what is being required of you, what is being done to you).

Step 3. Identify controllable and uncontrollable aspects of the situation (i.e., what can be changed, what can't be changed).

Step 4. Establish goals for coping based on the appropriate fit between coping strategies and appraisal of the situation (i.e., problem-focused strategies for controllable stressors, emotion-focused strategies for uncontrollable stressors).

Practicing Effective Coping

Complete the following exercise to practice Steps 1, 2, and 3 of the coping guidelines. First, think of a general stressful situation in your life (e.g., being infected with HIV). Then identify the specific demands of that general situation (e.g., having frequent doctor appointments, managing medication). Next identify what aspects of the problem are controllable (e.g., managing medication) and which ones are uncontrollable (e.g., having frequent doctor appointments).

Breaking Down Qualities of Stressors Exercise

1. Choose a general stressor: _____

2. Identify specific stressful demands:

 ▪ _____

 ▪ _____

 ▪ _____

■ _____

■ _____

■ _____

3. Separate controllable and uncontrollable aspects:

Controllable:

■ _____

■ _____

■ _____

Uncontrollable:

■ _____

■ _____

■ _____

Matching Coping Strategies to Stressors

After practicing Steps 1, 2, and 3, Step 4 is to choose an appropriate coping strategy. It is important to match the strategy to a specific aspect of the stressful situation. Remember that problem-focused coping is best used when attempting to deal with controllable stressors, and emotion-focused coping is better used when stressors are perceived as being uncontrollable. Keep in mind that some situations (e.g., talking to family members about HIV) may involve a mixture of controllable (e.g., what to say and when) and uncontrollable (e.g., how they react) aspects.

Steps to Problem-Focused Coping (for dealing with controllable stressors)

1. Brainstorm options for changing the situation.

2. Consider the possible outcomes of each option.

3. Order the options according to their level of importance.

Examples of Emotion-Focused Coping (for dealing with uncontrollable stressors)

- Do relaxation exercises

- Pursue pleasant activities

- Accept negative emotions instead of avoiding them

Coping Plan Exercise

Complete the following exercise to practice establishing productive coping plans.

Think of both a general personal situation and a situation related to HIV.

Personal Situation: _____

Controllable Stressor: _____

Problem-Focused Coping:

    1) Possible options: _____

    _____

    _____

    2) Outcomes of options: _____

    _____

    _____

    3) Priority of options: _____

    _____

    _____

Uncontrollable Stressor: _____

Emotion-Focused Coping: _____

_____

_____

HIV Situation: _____

Controllable Stressor: _____

Problem-Focused Coping:

  1) Possible options: _____

  _____

  _____

  2) Outcomes of options: _____

  _____

  _____

  3) Priority of options: _____

  _____

  _____

Uncontrollable Stressor: _____

Emotion-Focused Coping: _____

_____

_____

Softening Technique for Overwhelming Stressors

Sometimes you may encounter overwhelming or uncontrollable stressors that require an immediate response on your part to avoid remaining overwhelmed. One helpful immediate response is acceptance. You can use a technique known as "softening" to help you accept even the most stressful circumstances. Much of this technique involves changing your attitude toward unpleasant stimuli, thoughts, or feelings. Instead of bracing against or running away from feelings and experiences, you allow "what is" to be there. This frees up your energy to take in as much information as possible, deal with the reality of the situation, and maximize your options for coping.

Practicing Softening Against Pain

To soften around emotional pain, first become aware of an uncomfortable or distressing situation that you may have been avoiding. Just let the feelings associated with that situation flow into your body. Try to experience these feelings in a nonjudgmental way. Acknowledge the pain, and adopt an attitude of compassion towards the feelings associated with the pain. This will often bring a sense of release and self-acceptance.

RELAXATION TRAINING: *Autogenic Training with Imagery and Self-Suggestions*

Goals

- To practice autogenics with imagery and self-suggestions

- To practice sunlight meditation with autogenics

Autogenic Training with Imagery and Self-Suggestions

Adding visual imagery to your autogenic practice can enhance the relaxation experience. It can help turn your attention inward and give you the sense that you are going on an inner journey.

Positive self-suggestions are another addition to autogenic practice this session. At the end of a relaxation period, you are in a highly suggestible state. Repeating positive phrases to yourself at this time can help your efforts to achieve your goals or make positive changes. For example, if you want to stop smoking, you could use the positive self-suggestion, "I enjoy breathing pure air." Keep self-suggestions brief and to the point, as well as believable.

You may also want to try using suggestions that deepen relaxation and/or make you feel more centered. Examples include:

- I feel a deep sense of calm

- My whole body feels quite heavy, comfortable, and relaxed

- My mind is quiet; I feel serene and still

Autogenics with Visual Imagery and Positive Self-Suggestions Exercise

Repeat the autogenic exercises from Sessions 5 and 6. After repeating the formulas for heaviness and warmth and for heartbeat, breathing, abdomen, and forehead, move directly into the following exercise.

Breathe deeply, releasing tension with every exhalation. Do not hold onto your thoughts; just let them pass on by. As your mind becomes clear, feel yourself becoming calm and relaxed.

Imagine yourself moving further and further down into relaxation. As you reach the depth of your relaxation, find yourself surrounded by a calm, peaceful scene. Step into this scene and follow a path to a special place of your own choosing. This may be a place that you have been, or that you would like to go, or that exists only in your imagination.

Pick a comfortable spot and lie down, letting your body sink into the ground. Feel a sense of calm and relaxation. As you lie comfortable and relaxed, repeat your special phrase to yourself three times.

Continue with any positive self-suggestions or imagery that you find useful. To end the exercise, say to yourself three times, "I am relaxed and alert." Inhale deeply and exhale, letting go of any remaining tension. When you are ready, slowly open your eyes.

Sunlight Meditation with Autogenics

This exercise combines autogenics with sunlight imagery to create a sense of warmth and relaxation. To begin, imagine yourself in a scenic outdoor setting. The light of the sun gently shines down on you. You feel its warmth beginning to relax and soothe every part of your body.

Imagine that you are moving the sunlight to different parts of your body—each arm, each leg, abdomen, and chest—one by one. For each body part, imagine the sunlight shining down on it, warming and soothing the entire area. Feel that body part becoming completely relaxed, and then move the sunlight to the next body part.

When you have gone through each body part, take a moment to feel the sensations of warmth and relaxation across your chest, abdomen, arms, and legs. Focus on these sensations for a few minutes. To bring yourself out of deep relaxation to a more alert state, gradually let yourself become more aware of your surroundings, remaining calm and relaxed.

Homework

✎ Choose any of the types of relaxation taught so far in the program (i.e., PMR, breathing, imagery, autogenic training). Practice twice a day and record stress levels before and after on the Daily Self-Monitoring Sheet.

✎ Continue to monitor your stress levels at specified times each day and record on the Daily Self-Monitoring Sheet.

✎ Complete the Breaking Down General Stressors Exercise in this chapter.

✎ Complete the Coping Plan Exercise in this chapter.

✎ Record your coping responses to at least three separate stressful situations on the Matching Coping Behaviors and Appraisals Monitoring Sheet. For each situation, identify a specific aspect and indicate whether it is controllable or uncontrollable. Also list your coping behaviors according to whether they are productive or nonproductive and problem-focused or emotion-focused. Evaluate the match between the coping behavior and the appraisal of the specific aspect (i.e., problem-focused for controllable aspects, emotion-focused for uncontrollable aspects). You may photocopy this form from the book or download multiple copies from the Treatments *ThatWork*™ Web site at www.oup.com/us/ttw.

Matching Coping Behaviors and Appraisals Monitoring Sheet

Use this form to record situations that you have to cope with. Evaluate the match between the coping behavior and the appraisal of the specific aspect (problem-focused for controllable aspects, emotion-focused for uncontrollable aspects).

Situation	Specific Aspects Check "C" for controllable or "U" for uncontrollable	Coping Behavior Check the appropriate boxes: Productive: "P" Nonproductive: "N" problem-focused: "pf" emotion-focused: "ef"	Evaluate Match Check "M" for match or "X" for mismatch.	Modified Coping Modify your coping strategy if it does not match the appraisal of the specific aspect.
Decide to tell family about HIV status	Family's reaction C ☐ U ☑	P ☐ N ☑ pf ☑ ef ☐ Avoid seeing them	M ☐ X ☑	Softening technique
	C ☐ U ☐	P ☐ N ☐ pf ☐ ef ☐	M ☐ X ☐	
	C ☐ U ☐	P ☐ N ☐ pf ☐ ef ☐	M ☐ X ☐	
	C ☐ U ☐	P ☐ N ☐ pf ☐ ef ☐	M ☐ X ☐	
	C ☐ U ☐	P ☐ N ☐ pf ☐ ef ☐	M ☐ X ☐	
	C ☐ U ☐	P ☐ N ☐ pf ☐ ef ☐	M ☐ X ☐	

Chapter 9

Overview

Anger is the focus of the stress management portion of this session. You will become aware of your typical anger responses and patterns and learn better ways to manage your anger. The relaxation section of this session introduces meditation. You will practice mantra meditation, which involves repeating a syllable or word.

STRESS MANAGEMENT: *Anger Management*

Goals

- To learn about anger

- To become aware of your typical anger responses and patterns

- To learn anger management

Anger Responses

One aspect of stress management is learning how to deal with negative situations, including those in which one has been unfairly treated, slighted, or offended by others in some way. It is normal and reasonable to respond to these kinds of situations with anger. Healthy anger can motivate you to take actions to correct the situation. Less healthy anger, though, includes "stuffing feelings" on one extreme to "explosive responses" on the other.

The exercise on pages 84–85 will help you to better understand anger in both yourself and others. It will increase your awareness of how anger both positively and negatively affects you in your present life.

Self-Evaluation Questionnaire: Developing Awareness of Anger

Ask yourself the following questions:

1. What messages did you receive as a child about expressing anger?

   _____

   _____

   a. When my mother got angry, she: _____

   _____

   b. When my father got angry, he: _____

   _____

   c. When I got angry, I: _____

2. As a result of these experiences, what decisions have you made about anger and what it may mean in your life?

   _____

3. What types of people, situations, and events tend to make you angry now?

   _____

4. Is it ever OK for you to feel anger?

   It is OK to feel anger when: _____

   _____

5. How do you feel about expressing your angry feelings?

   When I get angry at someone, I: _____

   _____

6. How do you feel about other people expressing their anger?

   When someone gets angry with me, I: _____

   _____

7. When you express anger, how do you go about it? Are you aggressive? Assertive? Stubborn? Resistant? Complaining? Rebellious?

    _____

    _____

8. Do you turn anger in on yourself?

    I turn anger in on myself when: _____

    _____

9. What are you willing to do to increase your ability to recognize angry feelings, express anger, and communicate anger appropriately?

    _____

    _____

10. When have you used anger effectively?

    I have used anger effectively when: _____

    _____

11. What are the ways that anger has been a problem for you or has generated negative changes in your life?

    _____

    _____

12. What are the ways that anger has been empowering to you or has generated positive changes in your life?

    _____

    _____

13. What things do you like about the way you use anger, and what do you still want to change?

    _____

    _____

Anger and Awareness

It is important for you to become aware of your anger before it gets out of control. Once this happens, it is difficult to be analytical and objective about the situation.

Awareness of the Physical Symptoms of Anger

One of the easiest ways to become aware that you are angry about something is to become aware of your typical physical symptoms. For example, your heart might beat faster, your muscles may tense up, or your face may become red. By noticing these symptoms as they happen, you can become aware of your anger sooner and deal with it more effectively. Also, early awareness helps anger from building up, which can have a negative effect on your body (e.g., high blood pressure and increased muscle tension).

Awareness of Patterns of Responding

It is important to become aware of your typical patterns of responding to situations that induce anger. Study your Self-Evaluation Questionnaire to see if there are any patterns to your anger, where they might come from, and how effective they are. Think about how you feel after your usual anger responses and whether or not you want to change the way you respond.

Part of raising your awareness also includes being more aware of how your anger responses affect other people. Your response itself may trigger angry feelings in those around you. It can also have consequences for your relationship with them.

Awareness of the Power Dynamics of the Situation

Another step of awareness is recognizing your position of power in the situation.

The amount of power you hold can vary in different relationships (e.g., in your relationship with a boss versus with a colleague who is at an equal or subordinate position within the company). With persons who hold power over you, like the boss, the consequences of a confrontation may not be worth the potential benefits.

Also, in casual interactions with persons you are not likely to interact with again, the value of sharing personal feelings may not be worth the investment. In closer, more long-standing relationships, you may be more willing to express your feelings. The hope is that the person will change her behavior in the future of your continuing relationship.

Awareness of Other External and Internal Factors

Other factors may contribute to an aggravating situation. For example, you or the other person may be irritable because you are sick, tired, or hungry. You may be pushing each others' "buttons." There may be unresolved issues or other demands that are weighing on the situation. It is important to be aware of other internal and external factors when assessing the reasons for your or someone else's anger.

Anger Management

Now that you are aware of your typical symptoms and patterns of anger, you can begin to learn ways to slow down the automatic anger process and manage anger more effectively.

Slowing Down the Automatic Anger Process

- Recognize the thoughts you are having about the situation before you react. Do you feel offended by a person? Unfairly treated by a person or organization? Frustrated by a turn of events?

- Notice physical symptoms of anger—these are cues that you are being emotionally affected by the situation.

- Acknowledge your anger (don't invalidate your emotion). Attempting to suppress your anger will not alter the physical effects you are experiencing. Denial may also delay you from taking action to end the aggravating event or behavior.

- If you are too upset or angry to deal with situation appropriately, take time to cool down or use a buffer (e.g., exercise, talking it over) before dealing with the situation.

Anger Appraisal

You can use the process of cognitive restructuring learned in previous sessions to better manage anger. Practice examining your thought processes, identifying where distorted negative thoughts cause unnecessary anger, and changing these negative thoughts to more rational and realistic thoughts. Ask yourself the following questions:

- What are things I say to myself (thoughts) that make me angry?

- What is the valid part of my anger?

- Do I have any distorted thoughts contributing to or exacerbating my experience of anger? (e.g., "No one treats me with respect"; "Everyone steps on me.")

- What are more rational and realistic thoughts that may decrease my anger?

When angry at another person, it is important to respect and understand the other person's position. You may want to ask yourself the following questions:

- Where is the other person coming from?

- Is the other person "off the wall"?

- What might I be doing to make the other person angry?

- Is it possible that the other person might be right in her actions and I might be wrong in my interpretation of what is going on?

The following four steps (ASAP) can help you gain a better understanding of what is making you angry, what options you have for dealing with the anger, and managing the anger in an effective manner.

Questions to Ask Yourself ASAP

Awareness: Who or what am I really angry with or about?

Source: Why? What is the real source of my anger?

Alternatives: What do I want to do? Do I have alternatives for accomplishing the same thing?

Plan: What is my plan of action?

Expressing Anger: What Are Your Options?

In learning the best ways to express anger there are two main considerations. One concerns choosing a strategy; the other is having alternative options available.

Strategy Tips

- Recognize your needs

- Recognize the needs of the other person

- Assess timing (Do I need to be in a better mood to say something about this? Does the other person need to be in a better mood?)

- Establish the desired outcome (Do you want to salvage the relationship? Do you want to reach a certain goal no matter what it does to the relationship?)

- Determine the power differences in the relationship (Who holds the power in this situation? Are you above or below this person, or are you on equal footing?)

- Determine the nature of the continuing relationship (Are you close to this person? Will you have a future relationship with this person?)

Alternative Options to Stuffing Anger or Blowing Up

- Assertiveness (e.g., "When you do Y, I feel X.")

- Cooling down (i.e., waiting for a better time)

- Defusing (e.g., seeking advice)

- Exercise (e.g., going for a walk)

- Expression (e.g., informing the person that you think you are being treated unfairly)

- Information seeking (i.e., getting more details about the situation or what the person is communicating)

Recognizing and Changing Your Typical Anger Pattern

Answer the following questions to learn more about your typical anger pattern and how you respond to situations that induce anger.

1. What are the kinds of things that make you most angry over and over again? What pushes your buttons?

   _____

2. What is your characteristic physical reaction?

   _____

3. What are your characteristic emotions?

   _____

4. What is your characteristic coping response (problem-focused, emotion-focused)?

   _____

5. What are your characteristic behaviors?

   _____

6. What are better alternatives to dealing with your anger?

   _____

RELAXATION TRAINING: *Mantra Meditation*

Goals

- To learn about meditation

- To practice mantra meditation

Introduction to Meditation

Meditation involves focusing attention and awareness. Meditation allows you to have a quiet time to turn your attention within, to steady and center the mind, and to develop a quiet awareness. When you center yourself in this way, you can bring a sense of balance to all your activities. Meditation has also shown to have beneficial physical effects and has been used in treating many medical conditions.

The form of meditation practiced in this session is called *mantra meditation* and involves the repetition, either aloud or silent, of a syllable, a word, or a group of words like "one," "peace," "shalom," or "om." The mantra serves as the object of focus for the meditation. Repetition of your chosen mantra will help center your attention.

The Meditative Attitude

The meditative attitude is one of passive nonjudgmental witnessing. Thoughts should be treated like clouds floating by. Do not hold onto thoughts or engage with them; just let them go. When you find that your mind has drifted, gently bring the mind back to your mantra. This may happen again and again in the course of a meditation.

Choosing a Mantra

Select a syllable (e.g., "om"), a word (e.g., "one" or "peace"), or a short phrase (e.g., "I am calm") that you would like to use as a mantra. Once you have chosen a mantra, try to stick with it throughout your practice, as it will quickly come to be associated with the meditation experience.

Meditation Practice

Get into a comfortable position for meditation. Sit in a chair or cross-legged on the floor with a cushion underneath your seat so your knees touch the floor. Keep your back straight and upper torso balanced on your hips. Close your mouth and breathe through your nose. Rest your hands in your lap or place them open on your knees with your forefingers and thumbs touching.

Take several deep breaths and allow all of the day's activities and concerns to fall away. Do not hold on to any of them. Begin to focus on your breath, breathing slowly and naturally. Breathe away any thoughts that may be distracting or disturbing you.

Take a moment to scan your body and become aware of any held tension. Let go of any tension in any part of your body. Then shift your attention back to your breath, which has established its own regular and even pattern.

Begin to repeat your mantra over and over. Let your mantra find its own rhythm; do not force it. Focus on your mantra with minimal effort. If you observe any sensations in your body, just notice them, and then return to the repetition of your mantra. If you have any distracting thoughts, just notice them, and then bring your attention back to your mantra.

Maintain soft awareness of each repetition of your mantra. Remain in this state as long as you want, repeating your mantra at regular intervals until you are completely calm and relaxed. When you are ready to end your meditation, take a deep breath, exhale fully, and open your eyes. You can say to yourself, "I am refreshed and alert."

Benefits of Regular Practice

Regular practice is important to experience the maximum benefits of mediation. With continued practice, you can deepen your level of relaxation and sense of centeredness. You will become more skilled at experiencing thoughts, sensations, and events without overreacting to them. You can carry this skill into your daily life. When you first begin to meditate, the regularity of practice is most important. Practice every day, even if it is only for five minutes. As you become more practiced, 20 to 30 minutes once or twice a day is optimal.

Homework

✎ Practice mantra meditation on a daily basis (twice a day if possible). Record stress levels before and after each practice on the Daily Self-Monitoring Sheet.

✎ Continue to monitor your stress levels at specified times each day and record on the Daily Self-Monitoring Sheet.

✎ Review your answers to the Self-Evaluation Questionnaire: Developing Awareness of Anger.

✎ Review your answers to the exercise entitled "Recognizing and Changing Your Typical Anger Pattern."

✎ Use the Anger Awareness Monitoring Sheet to record the anger responses that you are most aware of in situations during the next week. You may photocopy this form from the book or download multiple copies from the Treatments *ThatWork*™ Web site at www.oup.com/us/ttw.

Anger Awareness Monitoring Sheet

Use this form to record situations which arouse anger and your responses to them. Think of healthy ways you can respond to these situations instead.

Situations Which Arouse Anger	Physical Response	Automatic Thoughts	Behaviors	Alternative Anger Response
Cut off while driving	Tense shoulders, heart beating faster	What a jerk! I shouldn't have let him by.	Honked horn. Yelled through the window.	Turn on the radio and enjoy some music while cooling down

Chapter 10

Session 9: Assertiveness Training / Breath Counting Meditation

Overview

The stress management section of this session teaches assertiveness. You will learn about different ways to communicate and identify your own interpersonal style. You will practice communicating effectively, as well as review possible obstacles and steps to behaving assertively. How to deal with conflicts using problem solving will also be discussed. For relaxation, you will learn a new meditation technique, breath counting.

STRESS MANAGEMENT: *Assertiveness Training*

Goals

- To learn about interpersonal styles
- To practice assertive communication
- To understand barriers to assertive behavior
- To use problem solving with conflicts
- To review steps to assertive behavior

Interpersonal Styles

Learning how to communicate effectively with others is a very important component of stress management training. There are several different interpersonal styles people can use to communicate. Some of these are less effective and more likely to cause conflict. The four basic interpersonal styles are described as follows. The pros and cons of each communication pattern are given.

Four Basic Interpersonal Styles

1. *Aggressive:* Standing up for one's rights by denying feelings of other people

   (+) *Advantage:* People usually don't push an aggressive person around.

   (−) *Disadvantage:* People avoid an aggressive person.

2. *Passive:* Indirectly violating one's own rights by failing to express honest feelings and beliefs

   (+) *Advantage:* Passive individuals rarely experience direct rejection.

   (−) *Disadvantage:* Other people end up making choices for the passive individual, making it hard for the individual to achieve personal goals. Passivity also leads to built-up resentment and guilt for not taking care of oneself.

3. *Passive-Aggressive:* Indirectly and passively resistant

   (+) *Advantage:* A passive-aggressive person avoids direct conflict.

   (−) *Disadvantage:* Passive-aggressiveness can often cause more interpersonal conflict than directly approaching a situation or person.

4. *Assertive:* Standing up for rights and expressing individual feelings and beliefs in a direct way that does not violate rights of others

   (+) *Advantage:* One can choose one's own goals, not turn people off, promote self-efficacy and self-esteem, and decrease interpersonal conflict.

   (−) *Disadvantage:* People who are less comfortable or familiar with the direct expression of feelings and desires may withdraw from or grow anxious or irritable during an exchange with an assertive person.

Practicing Alternative Assertive Responses

As you can see from the pros and cons, assertive communication is the most effective interpersonal style. Recall some of the situations role-played in the group meeting. Practice coming up with alternative assertive responses for each interpersonal communication.

Aggressiveness: You've purchased merchandise that is defective and you storm into the store on a busy Saturday afternoon and loudly complain to the salesperson and call him a liar.

Alternative Assertive Response: _____

_____

Passiveness: You are waiting in line and you are in a hurry and someone cuts in front of you. You do nothing.

Alternative Assertive Response: _____

_____

Passive-Aggressiveness: Someone asks to borrow some money from you. You are uncomfortable about this request but grudgingly agree to give him the money tomorrow. Tomorrow comes and you conveniently forget to bring the money with you.

Alternative Assertive Response: _____

_____

Barriers to Assertive Behavior

People tend to avoid using assertive behavior for two main reasons. One reason is that people often misinterpret what it means to be assertive—for example, thinking it means being pushy. Another main reason is that people have negative and inaccurate thoughts and beliefs that keep them from being assertive. Many of these kinds of thoughts, however, can be challenged and replaced. Here are some common examples of negative thinking and cognitive distortions that prevent assertive behavior:

Fear of Displeasing Others

When others disapprove of us, it may be unpleasant and uncomfortable. If we incorrectly interpret disapproval to mean that we are completely bad, we are more likely to become depressed and less likely to stand up for our rights.

Fear of Rejection or Retaliation

Often, we react to this fear by acting helpless. We forget that we do not have to passively accept inappropriate treatment. We can protect ourselves or we can do things for ourselves that would make the rejection easier to face.

Mistaken Sense of Responsibility

When we internalize others' hurt feelings, we take on the responsibility of making everyone else happy. When another person is hurt by your being assertive, it is important to determine whether you actually hurt the other person or whether the other person felt hurt because of his or her misinterpretation of your assertive behavior.

Mistaken View of Your Human Rights

Many people believe that they don't have the right to stand up for their wants, needs, and wishes. It is very difficult to be assertive when you are denying yourself basic rights. Remember, you can accept and act on your own rights without violating the rights of others.

Reluctance to Forfeit Advantages of Being Nonassertive

You may not want to give up the benefits of acting nonassertively. For example, if you don't stand up for your rights, others may defend you and you are still safe. Or by never disagreeing, you can appear to be easy to get along with. It is important to assess what you are giving up by acting assertively. Usually you will find that the benefits of assertiveness outweigh the costs.

Feeling Vulnerable and Unsafe

People who feel threatened and powerless often exhibit anger and aggression. It is important to be aware of situations in which you may feel vulnerable, making you more likely to lash out. By preparing yourself for these situations you can stay focused on any irrational thoughts that could cause you to communicate in an aggressive manner (e.g., "I don't get any respect"; "I need to show him that he can't mess with me").

Self-Check for Barriers to Assertive Behavior

Determine your personal barriers to assertive behavior by answering the following questions:

1. Did you identify with any of the common barriers to assertive behavior?

    _____

2. What are some of your reasons why you do not behave assertively?

    _____

3. When do you behave nonassertively? Any recent situations come to mind?

    _____

4. Are you able to predict the situations where nonassertive responses are more likely to occur in your life?

    _____

5. Who are the people with whom you act nonassertively? What is it about them or your expectation about them that affects the way you communicate?

    _____

There are several components to assertive communication. These are outlined as follows.

"I" Language

Messages in the "I" language are good ways to express negative feelings in a nonblaming way. When using these statements you can point out how others' behaviors concretely affect you while owning your own feelings about the situation. Compare the two examples.

Blaming "You" Message: "When you are late from work, you make me feel insecure."

Assertive "I" Message: "When you are late from work, I often doubt myself and feel insecure about the relationship."

"I Want" Statements

Clarify what you really want, which allows the other person to understand how to fulfill your wants. For example, "I want to eat dinner on time tonight."

"I Feel" Statements

Clarify how you feel without blaming or attacking the other person. Don't use generalizations to describe how you feel; instead, be specific and quantify your feelings (e.g., extremely happy, slightly irritated). For example, "I feel slightly irritated when you don't call to let me know you'll be late."

Empathic Assertion

This type of message contains two statements. The first statement recognizes the other person's situation, feelings, beliefs, and wants. The second statement asserts your wants, feelings, and beliefs. This message communicates sensitivity for the other person without a total disregard for your rights. For example, "I know that you have a lot of work and that it is difficult for you to guess when it will be done, but I need you to call if you are going to be late so I can organize my own schedule this evening."

Effective Listening

Effective listening is an important part of assertive communication. Listening to others often encourages others to listen to you more attentively. In addition, effective listening makes it less likely that you will misinterpret the message. Effective listening does not mean you are passively agreeing with the other person's message. Rather, you are respecting the rights of the sender to express his thoughts and feelings. Effective listening usually consists of two parts:

- *Paraphrasing* (summarizing) the content of the message

- *Nonverbal communication* that one is attentive (e.g., making eye contact, leaning forward, saying "uh huh")

Making Assertive Statements and Listening Effectively

Read over the following situations and answer the questions provided. This exercise will help you learn how to communicate assertively in different situations.

Situation 1

I have difficulty getting my partner to listen to me. He nods his head as if he is listening. However, when I ask for feedback, he has no idea what I just said. He doesn't pay attention unless I yell and scream, but, the more I get angry, the less he wants to listen.

What effective messages could you send to your partner?

_____

How can the partner communicate that he is listening?

_____

Situation 2

I have difficulty saying no to friends and family when they ask for favors. I don't want to come off as unfeeling. I find myself overextended because I always place others' needs before my own.

How can you assertively and confidently deny a request from others?

_____

How can you assertively respond when others deny your request for help?

_____

Situation 3

I was supposed to go out with a friend. At the last minute he called and canceled the appointment. This has been happening on a regular basis. I would really like to let him know that I am irritated with this behavior, but I really don't want to rock the boat and make matters worse.

How can you assertively criticize the behavior while still letting the person know you value the friendship?

_____

How can you assertively respond when others criticize your behavior?

_____

Situation 4

Can you think of a situation that occurred this week that involved some form of nonassertive communication?

_____

Were you able to come up with a more assertive alternative? How did you communicate this to the recipient?

_____

How did it go over? How did you feel afterwards?

_____

Sometimes you must deal with situations where the actual messages, desires, and feelings of yours and the other party are not clear. Were there any such situations like this that you found yourself in during the past week? If so, you can apply what you have learned about making assertive statements to problem-solving conflicts using the following steps:

1. Recognize there is a problem and define it in clear terms. Be specific and avoid generalizations.

2. Identify possible solutions. Both parties should generate a variety of possible solutions.

3. Critique each possible solution. It is important to be assertive, but remember that the best solution will meet both parties' needs.

4. Accept a solution. Both parties should discuss the expected outcomes and possible barriers to implementing the solution.

Barriers to Conflict Resolution

Many things can get in the way of a successful resolution; however, many of these barriers reflect *inaccurate beliefs* about conflict, such as:

- There is always a winner and a loser

- Direct conflict is to be avoided at all cost

- All conflicts must be resolved

- One person is all right; the other is all wrong

If you encounter this type of *self-talk* it can be challenged and replaced with more rational and less extreme statements. Here are some examples:

- Each person can walk away from a conflict having learned something

- Direct conflicts can take a lot of out you but are sometimes productive in taking care of things before they fester and turn into resentments

- Sometimes people just agree to disagree

- Usually neither person is 100% correct in a conflict

Unsolvable Problems

There may be situations in which no workable solution is available or the risk of being assertive is too great. Have you experienced any of these lately? What were they? Were you aware that an assertive response was not likely to help? In such cases there are alternatives to directly assertive behavior, such as changing your environment, developing ways of satisfying yourself, and tending to your emotional needs. You can also use the other coping strategies you have learned in this program (see Sessions 6 and 7 for techniques such as acceptance).

Steps to More Assertive Behavior

1. Be able to identify the four interpersonal styles: passive, passive-aggressive, aggressive, and assertive.

2. Identify situations in which you want to be assertive.

3. Plan for change:
   - Look at both your and the other person's rights, wants, and needs
   - Determine the desired outcome
   - Arrange a time and place to discuss the situation calmly

4. Define feelings using "I" messages. Express your request simply, firmly, and concisely.

5. Increase the possibility of getting what you want by being empathetic about the other person's position.

6. Use body language that conveys that you are attentive.

7. Learn to listen:
   - Make sure you are ready to listen
   - Listen and clarify what the other person said
   - Acknowledge what was said: communicate to the other person that you have heard his position

8. Be aware of barriers to assertive behavior, including counter-productive self-talk such as:
   - "My behavior will hurt someone else's feelings or they'll reject me"
   - "My job should be to make people happy and comfortable"
   - "In any conflict there has to be a winner and a loser"

RELAXATION TRAINING: *Breath Counting Meditation*

Goals

- To learn breath counting meditation

- To continue practicing meditation

Breath Counting Meditation

This meditation technique uses the breath as the object of focus. The basic technique is to count your breath from one to 10 on the exhale. To begin this meditation, get in a comfortable position. Take several long, deep breaths and begin to clear your mind. Let go of all the worries and concerns of the day. Close your eyes or fix them on a spot on the floor in front of you. You can either keep your eyes focused or let them go out of focus.

Take deep breaths and focus your attention on each part of the breath. First focus on the inhale. Then focus on the point at which you stop inhaling and start exhaling. Next focus on the exhale. Lastly focus on the pause between the exhale and the next inhale. Pay careful attention to the sensations in your body as you pause between breaths.

Begin to count your breaths on the exhale. Inhale . . . Exhale 1 . . . Inhale . . . Exhale 2 . . . Continue counting up to 10 and then start over at one. If any thoughts come to mind, just let them pass through you. Do not judge or engage with them; just allow them to come and go. If you lose your focus of attention, relax your breathing and start over at the count of one. If you start to lose count for any reason, just go back to the number one.

Try to repeat the counting sequence (inhale . . . exhale 1 . . .) for 20 minutes. If you'd like, you can add imagery related to the physical sensations of breathing and the feel and temperature of the inhalations and exhalations. You can focus on the flow of air through your nostrils: cool on the inhale and warm on the exhale. To end the meditation, bring your awareness back to the room at your own pace.

As you practice becoming more aware of your breath, more aware of yourself, the benefits of this practice will expand so that you can bring full attention to whatever you do during the rest of the day.

Homework

✎ Practice breath counting meditation on a daily basis (twice a day if possible). Record stress levels before and after each practice on the Daily Self-Monitoring Sheet.

✎ Continue to monitor your stress levels at specified times each day and record on the Daily Self-Monitoring Sheet.

✎ Complete the exercise in this chapter entitled "Practicing Alternative Assertive Responses."

✎ Complete the Self-Check for Barriers to Assertive Behavior.

✎ Review the exercise in this chapter entitled "Making Assertive Statements and Listening Effectively."

✎ Complete the Interpersonal Style Monitoring Sheet for each problem situation you encounter this week. You should try for a minimum of three situations. You may photocopy this form from the book or download multiple copies from the Treatments *ThatWork*™ Web site at www.oup.com/us/ttw.

Interpersonal Style Monitoring Sheet

Use this form to record problem situations and your responses. Follow the additional instructions in the column headings.

Situation	Automatic Thoughts Rate your belief in the thought (0%–100%)	Emotions Rate the intensity of your emotions (1–10)	Behavior Check the appropriate box: Aggressive: "A" Passive: "P" Passive-Aggressive: "PA" Assertive: "AS"	Alternative Assertive Response (if your behavior was nonassertive)
A friend owes me money.	He's always taking advantage of me: 50%	Anger: 6 Resentment: 7	A ☐ PA ☑ P ☐ AS ☐ I "forget" to bring money the next time we go out.	I ask him to pay for dinner to pay me back.
			A ☐ PA ☐ P ☐ AS ☐	
			A ☐ PA ☐ P ☐ AS ☐	
			A ☐ PA ☐ P ☐ AS ☐	
			A ☐ PA ☐ P ☐ AS ☐	

Chapter 11

Session 10: Social Support / Personal Stress Management Program

Overview

This is the final session of the program. You will learn the importance of social resources and evaluate your own social support network. You will identify any obstacles and learn stress management techniques for building and maintaining social support. You will also make plans for a personal stress management program. After the program has ended, you will need to continue practicing stress management skills and relaxation techniques on your own.

STRESS MANAGEMENT: *Social Support*

Goals

- To understand the benefits of social support

- To evaluate your social network

- To identify obstacles to maintaining strong social support

- To learn stress management techniques for maintaining social support

Understanding Social Support

Personal and Material Resources

When we think about resources, we often think about personal resources (for example, intelligence or sense of humor) and material resources (such as money, possessions). Our social resources, however, tend to enhance or detract from the importance we place on these other resources. Our relationships with other people can add to our enjoyment of these resources or can comfort us when we have a lack of resources. For example:

- Having other people to share our accomplishments (e.g., degrees, new house, job promotion) with is often what makes us feel so good about them

- Having others to console us during times of sorrow makes us feel less alone

- Having someone to laugh with when we tell a joke lets us know that our humor is appreciated

- Having someone to share our thoughts and ideas with lets us know that we are both appreciated and beneficial to other people

Think of your own examples of how social support enhances your life:

_____

_____

_____

Kinds of Social Support

There are four main kinds of social support:

- Emotional (e.g., people who you can share with and cry with)

- Tangible (e.g., people who you can catch a ride from or borrow money from)

- Informational (e.g., people who can provide information or give advice)

- Affiliative (e.g., people who you can have fun with, who share the same views as yours)

You may receive all four kinds of support from the same person or from different people in your social circle. Some support (especially involving informational support, a form of tangible support) comes from professionals such as doctors and nurses. You probably also provide support to others, which can make you feel good. Complete the questionnaire on pages 112–113 to help you to identify where your support networks' strengths and weaknesses exist. After completing the questionnaire, think about the people who provide you with support. Are these people available whenever you need them, or only some of the time? Are your interactions with these people (even the ones you love) always positive, or are they hurtful and disturbing at times?

Benefits of Social Support

Supportive relationships can have health-promoting effects on both our mental and physical well-being. Here are some examples of direct and indirect benefits of social support.

Direct Benefits

Informational Support (e.g., from doctors and nurses, HIV-infected individuals)

- Promotes healthier behaviors

- Facilitates your ability to obtain necessary medical care

- Provides guidelines for helping you adhere to your medications

- Provides advice leading to solutions

Tangible Support (e.g., from friends and family)

- Helps accomplish chores

- Provides money to pay bills

- Provides assistance to meet various obligations

- Provides transportation or childcare to allow you to attend medical appointments

Social Support Network Questionnaire

1. Whom in your life do you feel comfortable with sharing your thoughts and feelings both positive and negative?

Initials	Example of Support	Initials	Example of Support
JS	can complain to		

2. Whom can you count on to lend you a hand when you need it (e.g., getting a ride somewhere, doing chores, moving furniture, etc.)?

Initials	Example of Support	Initials	Example of Support
TR	helps get groceries		

3. Whom could you borrow money or significant items from if you needed it?

Initials	Example of Support	Initials	Example of Support
KP	gave loan to pay bills		

4. Whom could you get important information from if you needed it?

Initials	Example of Support	Initials	Example of Support
CW	help with insurance forms		

continued

5. Whom are the people you most enjoy spending your time with (these will probably be the people who make you feel most positive about yourself)?

Initials	Example of Support	Initials	Example of Support
FW	praises me		

6. Who do you feel truly cares about you and would be supportive of you under almost any circumstance?

Initials	Example of Support	Initials	Example of Support
CM	helped me when sick		

7. In what ways do you provide other people with support?

Initials	Example of Support	Initials	Example of Support
JL	make dinner for		

Indirect Benefits

Emotional Support (e.g., from friends and family)

■ As a coping resource, helps you redefine a stressor as being less overwhelming

■ Reduces your negative emotional reaction to events, allowing you to take positive actions

■ Allows you to vent fears and to lessen private worrying (which can decrease anxiety and depression and possibly reduce stress hormone levels)

Informational Support (e.g., from family, friends, HIV-infected individuals)

■ Provides information that can be used to challenge irrational cognitive appraisals (e.g., catastrophizing, all-or-nothing thinking)

Tangible Support (e.g., from doctors and nurses)

■ Helps with tasks that would be very difficult or impossible to accomplish on your own (e.g., navigating the health insurance system for reimbursement for medical care)

Affiliative Support (e.g., from friends and family)

■ Provides a sense of well-being, belongingness, purpose, and meaning

■ Gives you a greater sense of personal control over life events

■ May have positive physiological effects, such as better-regulated stress hormone levels

Obstacles to Maintaining Strong Social Support

Now that you understand the importance of social support for your mental and physical health, spend some time identifying any obstacles that stand in the way of your establishing or maintaining a solid social network.

See the following examples and check the obstacles that apply to your life. Rate each for its degree of controllability on a scale of one (low control) to four (high control). Then list other obstacles that prevent you from maintaining a strong social network and rate these.

Examples of Potential Obstacles   **Rating**

_____ Death of several family members or friends   _____

_____ Sickness of friends causing them to limit social activities   _____

_____ Fractured family ties   _____

_____ Self-imposed social withdrawal due to fears (of contagion, stigma, reminders of others who have gotten sick)   _____

_____ Sense of disconnection from past pre-HIV life and relationships   _____

_____ Other people fearing to be close (emotionally or physically) to an HIV-infected person   _____

Other Obstacles   **Rating**

_____   _____

_____   _____

_____   _____

_____   _____

_____   _____

Stress Management Techniques for Maintaining Social Support

Challenging Cognitive Appraisals

Quite often, our own cognitive distortions get in the way of starting or maintaining healthy relationships with other people. Answer the following questions to help you identify your irrational thoughts about relationships and challenge them.

1. What is your rationale for withdrawing from other people?

   _____

2. How else might your family, friends, co-workers, and potential friends and partners react to you if you gave them a chance?

   _____

3. How might you respond differently to people so as to gain their trust and improve your relationship with them?

   _____

4. How might you be more open and honest with people about your life in an effort to increase your level of intimacy with them?

   _____

Model of Awareness, Appraisal, Coping, and Resources

Figure 11.1 demonstrates the place of social resources in the stress management model.

Modifying Coping Strategies

The following strategies involve your social network and include examples of both problem- and emotion-focused productive coping.

- Seek out information (as it relates to your medical condition)
- Seek out tangible aid (money, advice, instructions)
- Communicate needs and feelings (positive and negative) more effectively to friends, family, and supportive others (e.g., medical personnel)
- Allow yourself to rely on trusted friends
- Enjoy the feeling of being nurtured by loved ones
- Express feelings (even anger) assertively
- Find a primary confidant (e.g. intimate partner, close friend, psychotherapist, support group, religious leader) and increase your connection to her

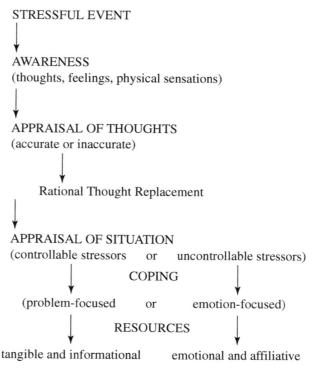

STRESSFUL EVENT

AWARENESS
(thoughts, feelings, physical sensations)

APPRAISAL OF THOUGHTS
(accurate or inaccurate)

Rational Thought Replacement

APPRAISAL OF SITUATION
(controllable stressors   or   uncontrollable stressors)

COPING

(problem-focused   or   emotion-focused)

RESOURCES

tangible and informational   emotional and affiliative

Figure 11.1

Model of awareness, appraisal, coping, and resources

▪ Increase involvement in the community (lending support to others)

▪ Keep a journal of positive interactions you have had with others and how this made you feel

▪ Consider getting a pet

Steps to Support Network Modification

The following steps can be used as a guide for changing or improving aspects your social support network.

Step 1. Identify support network strengths and weaknesses.

Step 2. Rate controllability of obstacles to forming and maintaining network.

Step 3. Challenge cognitive appraisals blocking supportive connections.

Step 4. Modify and execute various coping strategies.

Step 5. Re-evaluate the situation to see if it has improved.

PERSONAL STRESS MANAGEMENT PROGRAM

Goals

- To review the program

- To plan for home relaxation practice

- To establish a personal stress management program

Review of the Program

During this 10-week program, you have learned a variety of techniques for increasing awareness of how stress affects your life and ways that you can better manage your response to stressors.

Throughout the program, a primary goal has been the identification, or *awareness*, of stressors that you commonly encounter and the corresponding emotional, cognitive, behavioral, social, and physical symptoms of stress you typically experience as a result of these stressors.

The next step was to determine how your thoughts, or *appraisals*, of stressors lead to various stress symptoms. You were introduced to the concept of cognitive restructuring as a strategy for changing distorted negative thoughts into more rational and realistic thoughts that would help you to perceive and think about the world in a healthier manner.

Several sessions were then spent examining coping strategies and determining where they serve you well and not so well. Where you were using less productive coping strategies, you began changing them to more active strategies. You also learned that problem-focused strategies might serve best in controllable situations, but emotion-focused strategies might work better in uncontrollable situations. To help cope with other people, you examined better ways to manage your anger and also learned how to express yourself assertively.

Finally, you examined the important resources that you rely on in life, specifically social support. You considered how different people in your life serve different support functions (tangible, informational, emotional, affiliative). You then determined how you could improve your ability to establish and maintain strong social support networks.

Each of these goals was accomplished by learning a variety of techniques designed to facilitate a certain component of stress management.

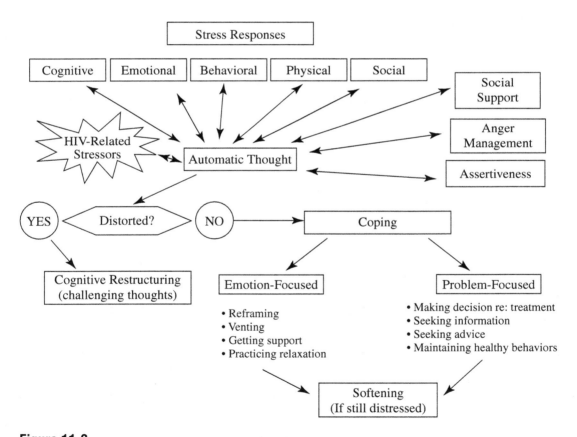

Figure 11.2

Model of CBSM for HIV-infected individuals

GOAL	TECHNIQUE
Awareness	PMR, body scan, meditation, breathing, imagery, autogenics
Appraisal	Cognitive restructuring
Coping	Productive coping skills, anger management, assertiveness
Resources	Social network, relaxation techniques

Each of these goals and activities is connected with the others, creating a complete stress management package. For many stressors, drawing upon several interrelated techniques at once provides the most efficient and productive strategy. Refer to figure 11.2 for an overview of the techniques available to you.

Planning for Home Relaxation Practice

As this is the last session, it is important for you to have a plan for continuing relaxation practice on your own. You should have a regular time and place for daily practice. Choose the exercises that you found most beneficial during the program and incorporate these into your relaxation practice. Make any modifications necessary for home practice.

Remember that instructions for all the relaxation exercises are included in this workbook. This allows you to read through the instructions and then simply close your eyes and guide yourself through the experience. It might take several practice attempts until you feel comfortable guiding yourself through the exercise with no help from the group leader. With continued practice, however, you should have no difficulty at all doing the exercises on your own.

If you do experience difficulties using this approach, you can try recording yourself reciting the relaxation scripts and then playing this back whenever you wish to do an exercise. Using headphones when listening to the recording during the exercise works best as it minimizes ambient sounds. For easy use, place the recording and playing device in the place where you plan to practice.

Congratulations on completing the program! You have made important accomplishments over the past 10 weeks. To maintain your "stress management fitness" you must continue using the techniques learned in this program, just as you would have to continue exercising to maintain physical fitness. Answer the following questions to help develop and maintain your personal stress management program:

1. How do you plan to integrate stress management into your life?

   _____

2. Do you feel that you are able to call upon the stress management tools you've learned? How so?

   _____

3. Do you have a plan for a regular program of relaxation? What exercises will you use? When? Where?

   _____

4. How will you begin this week? What tools will you use?

   _____

5. How will you review and continue to hone your skills in the future?

   _____

6. Where can you find support for living with HIV? What resources are available to you? How will you access them?

   _____

About the Authors

Michael H. Antoni, Ph.D., is Professor of Psychology and Psychiatry and Behavioral Sciences at the University of Miami and Program Leader at the Sylvester Comprehensive Cancer Center, and has been a licensed psychologist in the State of Florida since 1987. Dr. Antoni leads the Biobehavioral Oncology, Epidemiology, Prevention and Control research program, which includes over 20 faculty from the departments of Psychology, Psychiatry, Epidemiology, Medicine, and Microbiology/Immunology working together on transdisciplinary research projects. Dr. Antoni also serves on the graduate faculty in both the Clinical Health Psychology doctoral program and the Cancer Biology doctoral program at the University of Miami.

Dr. Antoni has led multiple NIMH-funded randomized controlled trials examining the ability of group-based cognitive behavioral stress management (CBSM) interventions to enhance psychological adjustment and modulate immune system functioning and health outcomes in HIV-infected men and women. He also serves as co-director of an NIMH pre- and post-doctoral training program in behavioral immunology and AIDS. He is also director of the National Cancer Institute (NCI)-funded Center for Psycho-Oncology Research (CPOR), one of the five mind-body centers funded by the NIH at the turn of the century. In the CPOR he directs a set of coordinated clinical trials and core laboratories that examine the effects of CBSM on psychosocial, endocrine, and immune functioning and the development of cervical carcinoma in women infected with HIV and human papillomaviruses (HPV) and on quality of life, endocrine and immune processes, and health status in women with breast cancer and men with prostate cancer. He has also served continuously as Principal Investigator for the past 14 years on an NCI-funded program of research in breast cancer that has demonstrated the efficacy of CBSM in three different randomized trials.

He has published over 380 journal articles, abstracts, chapters, and books in the area of stress management and health psychology, including *Stress Management for Women with Breast Cancer*. He is associate editor of the *International Journal of Behavioral Medicine* and *Psychology and Health* and serves on the editorial boards of *Health Psychology, Brain, Behavior and Immunity,* and *Annals of Behavioral Medicine*.

Gail Ironson, M.D., Ph.D., is Professor of Psychology and Psychiatry at the University of Miami and is a Board Certified Psychiatrist. She received her Ph.D. from the University of Wisconsin and her M.D. from the University of Miami, followed by residency training in Psychiatry at Stanford. She has over 150 publications in the areas of behavioral medicine, Psychoneuroimmunology, stress and coping with chronic illness (especially HIV), and examining psychological and biological factors that protect the health of people with HIV. She has been P.I. (Principal Investigator), Project Leader, or Co-P.I. on NIH-funded grants continuously for the past 18 years since she finished her residency training. A significant part of her research has been involved with implementing and examining the effects of cognitive-behavioral stress management with Mike Antoni and Neil Schneiderman in HIV. She also set up and has co-directed the Trauma Treatment program at the University of Miami for the past 10 years.

Notable accomplishments also include being President of the Academy of Behavioral Medicine Research in 2002 and being awarded the Alumni Professor Award for outstanding scholarship and teaching by the University of South Florida (Tampa). She is or has been on the editorial boards of five journals (*International Journal of Behavioral Medicine, AIDS and Behavior, Health Psychology, Journal of Applied Psychology, Journal of Disaster Psychiatry*). She is currently the recipient of two NIH-funded R01s ("Psychobiological Processes and Health in HIV" and "Efficacy of an Emotional Disclosure Intervention in HIV") and a grant from the Templeton/Metanexus foundation to study spirituality in HIV.

Neil Schneiderman, Ph.D., is James L. Knight Professor of Health Psychology, Psychiatry and Behavioral Sciences, and Medicine at the University of Miami. He is Director of the University's Behavioral Medicine Research Center and Director of the Division of Health Psychology in the Department of Psychology. Dr. Schneiderman is the Director of both an NIH Program Project and a Research Training Grant from the National Heart, Lung and Blood Institute on biobehavioral bases of cardiovascular disease risk and management. He is also Principal Investigator of the NIH Multi-Center Hispanic Community Health Study as well as an NIMH Research Training Grant on psychoneuroimmunology and HIV/AIDS. Dr. Schneiderman has led multiple randomized controlled trials examining the effects of group-based cognitive-behavioral stress management on psychological adjustments and biological outcomes in the areas of HIV/AIDS, prostate cancer, and cardiovascular disease and has published more than 300 refereed articles. His honors include Distinguished Scientist Awards from both the American Psychological Association and the Society of Behavioral Medicine and the Outstanding Scientific Achievement Award from the International Society of Behavioral Medicine.

CPSIA information can be obtained
at www.ICGtesting.com
Printed in the USA
BVOW07s1342230617
487467BV00011B/22/P